Peace Begins With Me

Peace

Begins

With Me

*An inspirational journey
to end suffering and restore joy*

by

Ted Kuntz, M.Ed

Published and Printed in Canada
Copyright 2005 by Ted Kuntz
201–3041 Anson Ave. Coquitlam
British Columbia, Canada V3B 2H6
First printing – June 2005
Second printing – May 2006

Canadian Cataloguing-in-Publication Date

Kuntz, Ted

Peace Begins With Me / Ted Kuntz

ISBN 0-9736669-0-0

1. Peacemaking   2. Self-improvement

Edited by Norine Webster
Cover design, design, layout and typography
by Lee Johnson

To all the people who want to create
a better life together

Contents

Contributors   9

Foreword   13

Introduction   15

Chapter One
The Tale of Two Wolves   23

Chapter Two
My Story   25

Chapter Three
Feeding the Negative Wolf   37

Chapter Four
Feeding the Positive Wolf   77

Chapter Five
Personal Action Plan   187

Chapter Six
Peace Begins With Me   195

Bibliography   201

About the Author   205

Peace Begins With Me

Contributors

In any project many people contribute to its creation. I'm grateful to the following people for their contributions to the development and evolution of this book and the ideas contained here:

Lee Johnson, Norine Webster, Hannah Diamond, Ross Buchanan, Al Etmanski, Vickie Cammack, Darlene Fletcher, Suzanne Kyra, Ray Woollam, Neale Donald Walsch, Nelson Mandela, Albert Einstein, Joshua Kuntz, Lani Anthony, Cathy Anthony, Gandhi, Dr. John Travis, Native culture, Werner Erhard, Byron Katie, Peter Ruetz, Tom Kuntz, Eckhart Tolle, Dr. Kevin Farrell, Mark Twain, Michael Warren, Don Miguel Ruiz, Rumi,

Hans Selye, Jerome Bouvier, Shakespeare, Dead Sea Scrolls, Buddha, Jeff Leach, Anthony Robbins, Dean Inge, Lowry Olafson, Abraham Lincoln, Lynn Grabhorn, David Morehouse, Spencer Johnson, Ron and Teresa Bourassa, Oprah Winfrey, Henry David Thoreau, Stephen Covey, God, and many others.

I hope you are as proud of this book as I am.

Ted Kuntz

*"It is no longer good enough to cry peace.
We must act peace, live peace, and march in peace, in alliance with the people of the world.*

Chief Shenandoah,

Six Nations Iroquois Confederacy

Peace Begins With Me

Foreword

In pursuit of my goal of making this world a better place, I have been fortunate to encounter a few exceptional companions – people who are gentle, kind, caring, and genuinely concerned about others and the environment.

Ted Kuntz is all these – and more.

What sets Ted apart from many others is he walks his talk. As long as I have known Ted, he has been on a quest of self-improvement. Yet, this improvement is not confined to the realm of personal growth. Ted also participates voraciously in his community's affairs. When there is a call for volunteers, Ted steps forward. When there is a worthy cause, Ted is there offering his time and talents, and if necessary, digging into his own pocket.

It has been a privilege to share some small encounters with Josh, and to watch Ted overcome his challenges and manifest a peaceful reality for himself. If I have in any small way helped or played a positive role, I am blessed tenfold in return by Ted's friendship.

My heartfelt wish is that Ted's book inspires everyone who reads it, and fills them with even a small measure of the love and compassion Ted and Josh share.

Lee Johnson
Vancouver, Canada

*Lee Johnson is a writer, designer, and co-author of **The Quest for the Corporate Soul** and the #1 best seller **How to Escape Your Comfort Zones***

Introduction

For centuries, possibly millennia, people have cried out for peace. Yet, we continue to be surrounded by conflict and war. Why is it that the peace we so desperately yearn for continues to elude us? What prevents mankind from experiencing true and lasting peace?

The common understanding is that governments are responsible for creating peace on earth. I believe nothing could be further from the truth.

Philosophers, saints, and sages from the beginning of time have greeted us with the phrase, *"Peace be with you"*. But, what does this mean? What does this expression tell us about finding peace? To me, it means peace must begin in my own heart and mind. In order to experience peace in the global world, I need to experience it first in my personal world. Peace begins at home. *Peace begins with me.*

This is the purpose of this book – to develop and nurture the attitudes, beliefs, and behaviors to enable peace to flourish *within*.

Many people assume we know what is required for peaceful co-existence. I believe otherwise. It is my observation that we are socialized to behave in competitive and controlling ways, rather than peaceful and cooperative ways.

As an example, consider the game of "musical chairs". This is a game played almost religiously at children's parties and other gatherings where young children are present. It is a simple game. Chairs are placed back-to-back in a row. The number of chairs is one less than the number of children participating. To begin, the children dance around the chairs while music is played.

When the music stops, the children are to find a chair and sit on it. Given there are insufficient chairs, one child will be without. The child who fails to obtain a seat is out of the game. Another chair is removed, and the game continues.

What philosophy is this game based on? What skills are encouraged? What experience is being created? In my experience, first as a participant, and more recently as the facilitator of this game, I've consistently witnessed the following outcome – one happy winner, and many unhappy losers. Usually the strongest, fastest, and most aggressive child wins, while the gentle and considerate are the first to lose.

It appears two premises underlie this game. One, there is not enough to go around. And two, nice people finish last. Charles Darwin might be pleased with a game based on a survival-of-the-fittest theme. I, however, think it is time we ask, *"Does this game reflect the kind of community we wish to create for ourselves? Are the skills of aggression and competition the ones we want our children to master?"*

Consider the potential impact were this game played by a different set of rules. What if a chair is removed every round as before, but this time the children must find a way they can all sit on the diminishing number of chairs? What might be the outcome of a game where creativity and cooperation are the ingredients to success, a game where no one is excluded for not being good enough or strong enough? What kind of qualities would this game nurture in our children? What kind of a society might these children create when they become its teachers, politicians, and business leaders?

An increasing number of books are being written on the topic of peace. This is a good thing. Most, however, are based on the assumption the reader already knows what peace is. I'm not certain this is true. I'm not confident that most children or adults know what peace is or have enjoyed consistent and prolonged peace. As a result, I believe the first requirement is to provide individuals with the information they require to *create* peace. I believe it is important to teach the beliefs, skills, and attitudes that allow peace to be readily experienced.

This book was birthed out of my own experience of searching for peace. I have a son named Joshua. Joshua was born healthy, but became disabled early in life due to the toxic effects of a childhood vaccine. For years I held the belief his disability was unacceptable. I experienced significant hurt, anger, and fear. I spent the first five years of Joshua's life in a state of war. I was angry at the world. I lashed out at others. I was miserable. I ached for peace, but the possibility felt far, far away. I believed I could experience peace and joy only if my son's condition improved. In the meantime, I felt powerless.

Then, one day, I had an epiphany. I came to the realization I needed to accept my son just as he is. This meant accepting his disabilities. I learned to appreciate there were gifts in this turn of events, valuable lessons for me to learn. Gradually my firmly entrenched beliefs and attitudes began to shift. I discovered a new way to see my son's condition and myself. This change finally allowed me to experience peace and joy again.

I discovered peace is within reach if I allow my beliefs and attitudes *within* to change. Previously, peace was possible only if my *external* world was in alignment with my expectations. I now appreciate the undue burden this belief placed on my desire for inner peace. In retrospect I see how a person's capacity for peace is often hindered by a belief system that focuses on the *external* world rather than the *internal* world. Gandhi captured the secret of peaceful living beautifully when he said, *"Be the change you want the world to be."*

My dream is to assist you to experience lasting peace. I believe that in doing so, our capacity to share this planet in peace and harmony will increase. This is my ultimate goal. This is my intention – Peace on Earth.

*We must pursue peaceful ends
through peaceful means.*

Martin Luther King Jr.

Peace Begins With Me

Chapter One

The Tale of Two Wolves

A Native elder walks slowly down the path. The leaves of the trees and the soft breeze protect him from the heat of the noonday sun. In his worn, calloused hand is the soft flesh of his young grandson. The two walk in silence.

After a time, the grandfather interrupts the silence. *"Grandson,"* he begins, *"There are two wolves fighting in my heart. One wolf is angry and vindictive, and wishes to hurt others. The other wolf is peaceful, joyful, and loving."*

Hearing the words of his grandfather, the grandson is filled with fear. With a tremor in his voice he asks, *"Grandfather, which wolf will win the battle of your heart?"*

The wise elder replies, *"The battle of my heart will be won by the wolf that wins the battle of every man's heart. It will be the wolf I feed."*

Chapter Two

My Story

I have a son named Joshua. Joshua is a young man who has finally reached the age of adulthood. His life has not been easy.

Joshua was born healthy. I remember his birth as if it happened yesterday. I remember the early morning phone call from the nurse who said, *"Your wife is ready to give birth. Come quickly."* Driving as fast as I could, I arrived at the hospital to find my wife fully immersed in the process of delivering our son.

As his mother released him from her womb, the light shimmered on Joshua's wet skin. The physician held Josh in his hands, examined him briefly, then with a smile placed my son in my outstretched arms. With deep penetrating eyes, Josh took in his first view of the world. It was a precious moment. A moment filled with peace and joy.

The peace and joy was not to last. When Josh was five months old, he began convulsing. The convulsion continued for more than 25 minutes. It was the longest 25 minutes of my life. Something ugly was happening to my son. Josh's mother and I rushed him to the nearest Emergency. Once there, the physician treated Josh with anti-convulsant medication, then discharged us with these words: *"Treat your son as a normal child, and everything will be fine."*

Unfortunately, everything wasn't fine. Less than one month after the first seizure, Josh seized for a second time. I would later learn that toxins from a recently administered childhood vaccine were the cause of these convulsions. This admission to hospital resulted in even more medications being prescribed.

For a few weeks everything seemed to return to normal. Then Josh seized again. And again. And again. Despite numerous medications and combinations of medications, the convulsions persisted. The interval between the seizures became shorter and shorter. By Josh's fourth birthday, he was seizing at a rate of twelve to fifteen times each day.

This was the most difficult time in my life. I was in agony every time my son seized. Knowing any one seizure had the potential to kill him further intensified my terror. The doctors explained that a seizure of the severity and duration experienced by my son expended as much energy as someone running a marathon. My four year old was running the equivalent of twelve to fifteen marathons every day!

The intense seizure activity caused tremendous damage to his developing brain. Most days the episodes left Josh too weak to walk, talk, or feed himself. His care became too demanding for his caregivers. As a result his mother was required to resign her job and provide full time care. Josh's sister Lani, who is five years older, was forgotten in the chaos. There simply wasn't enough time or energy to attend to the demands of a healthy nine-year old.

During Josh's fifth year the doctors at the Children's Hospital informed us they would no longer treat our son. They confided there was nothing else they could do to improve his condition. If we needed time away from Josh they would admit him to the hospital, but would no longer provide medical intervention. From their perspective Joshua's case was closed.

Words cannot express the pain I felt. I loathed watching my son seize over and over. It was unbearable to have the ongoing reminder of just how powerless I was to protect my son from harm. I lived in a state of constant dread. I feared Josh would die or become disabled beyond recognition. I resented the doctors for what their medicine had done to my son. I was angry they weren't able to correct their mistake and make him better. Waking each morning, knowing I was to face another day of seizing, tears, and helplessness, became an unbearable struggle. Thoughts of suicide visited me frequently. This caused even more guilt and pain. I hated my life. I felt trapped. I felt hopeless. I doubted I would ever be happy again.

In my profession as a family therapist I counsel troubled people. Yet I couldn't get my own life to work. I felt like a fraud. The knowledge and skills that I acquired as part of my professional training were inadequate to provide relief. I was desperate. Something had to change.

Out of my despair I did something I had never done before. I consulted a psychic. The psychic requested I come to the consultation with specific questions. I had only one question, *"Will my son live?"*

The psychic paused briefly and then replied, *"Have no fear, the son will outlive the father as he should."*

Shock and delight flooded me. The prediction that my son would live caused a tremendous stirring in my heart. Out of a renewed sense of hope, a second question arose.

"If my son is to live, what will he be when he grows up?"

Again the psychic paused, and then replied, *"Your son will be what he already is, and that is a teacher."*

A teacher? My son a teacher?

I was confused and in retrospect even angry. How could my son be a teacher? His intellectual capacity had been reduced to the level of a two year old! I immediately dismissed this notion. My son being a teacher just didn't seem possible.

After a time, however, I noticed curiosity growing inside of me. *If Josh is a teacher, then what might he teach me?* This question caused me to look at my son in a different way, to look deeper. Simply opening my mind to the possibility that Josh could teach me something allowed me to receive his lessons.

Josh's First Lesson

The circumstances surrounding my first lesson were rather unremarkable. Yet, while seemingly insignificant at the time, I now consider this one of the events that changed my life.

Like many fathers and sons, Josh and I shared a daily ritual. When I came home from work and drove up the driveway of our home, Josh would recognize the sound of my car and know I had arrived. If Josh was having a good day, a day with relatively few seizures, he'd run to the window facing the garage to watch me get out of the car. When I looked to the window I'd see his little nose pressed against the glass. With a joyful eagerness Josh would yell, *"Hi Dad."*

I'd wave, and return the greeting. This was a moment of shared joy. A moment I relished. On most days, however, the window was empty. Josh's absence meant he was either in seizure or having a particularly challenging day. I dreaded seeing an empty window.

Over time I noticed my stomach churning as I turned into the driveway of our home. I now realize it was the churning of fear as I anxiously considered the kind of day my little boy might be having. Would Josh's little nose be pressed against the glass, or would I find an empty window? Is Josh having a good day, or is it another day filled with seizures?

On this particular day I looked to the window as I faithfully did after parking my car. Framed in the window I saw Josh's smiling face. I paused to enjoy the relief I felt whenever I saw him there. As I basked in the warmth of my son's welcome, a question occurred to me. It was as though the question were spoken out loud.

Peace Begins With Me

The question I heard was, *"When your son looks out the window at you, what does he see?"*

In that brief moment of reflection I realized that my son saw a father who was angry and afraid, a father who was anxious and agitated, and a father who refused to accept his own child the way he is. In this moment of clarity, I knew my son deserved better.

That day I made a commitment.

I committed myself to doing whatever it took to become more peaceful, joyful, and happy. More importantly, I resolved to love the son I have, rather than the son I don't have. I released the son who only existed in my imagination – the healthy, normal son I knew before the onset of the seizures.

That day I began the most important journey of my life.

I began to experiment with life. I read extensively. I participated in far-ranging discussions.

I considered all kinds of ideas and actions. As I did so, one question guided me: *Do these thoughts and actions point me in the direction of peace, joy and happiness, or do they point me in the direction of anger, sadness and despair?* Later, I came to ask this question based on the Native story in Chapter One – *"Do these thoughts and actions feed the negative wolf, or the positive wolf?"*

This book is a summary of what I learned. In Chapter Three I describe the ideas and actions I came to understand point me in the direction of anger, sadness and despair, that feed the negative wolf. In Chapter Four I describe the ideas and actions that point me in the direction of peace, joy and happiness, that feed the positive wolf.

You might rightfully ask whether these ideas and actions will point you in similar directions. In truth I don't know that answer. Only you can know this by considering these ideas and trying the actions for yourself, and noticing the direction they point you in.

My intention in writing this book is to share with you the wisdom I acquired during my journey with my son so that you too might come to understand the source of your pain, and perhaps acquire ideas and strategies that enable you to experience a better life, a life in which peace and joy are very real possibilities.

It is my genuine desire that you acquire the tools to help you experience the inner peace, joy and happiness you truly deserve. Then my journey and Joshua's struggle will have been even more worthwhile.

Peace Begins With Me

Chapter Three

Feeding the Negative Wolf

Life with my son has offered me many opportunities to understand the various ways in which my thoughts and actions led me towards anger, fear and grief. I came to recognize that many of my beliefs, thoughts, and behaviors pointed me away from peace and happiness and fed my negative wolf. Because these were things I did, they were things I could change.

Outlined below is a description of six ways I

fed my negative wolf. I invite you to consider these ideas and notice whether they affect your capacity to experience peace, joy and happiness.

Ways I Fed My Negative Wolf:

1. Imagining the worst.

2. Making mistakes.

3. Thinking like a victim.

4. Living in the past or the future.

5. Resisting reality.

6. Delaying happiness.

1. Imagining the worst

When confronted with a situation where the outcome was unknown, I noticed I often responded by imagining the worst possible outcomes. I suspect this habit had something to do with the belief I was preparing myself to handle any difficulty that might arise.

When I became more observant of my thoughts and behaviors and the direction they point me in, I discovered a serious problem with this strategy. When I imagined the worst possible outcomes I experienced intense fear and anxiety. My heart would pound rapidly and my thoughts would race out of control. I noticed it was irrelevant whether what I imagined eventually occurred. Simply *thinking* a negative outcome caused significant emotional and physical distress.

Medical research confirms my observations. The physical body does not distinguish between a *real* event and an *imagined* event. The effect is the same. Thus, by imagining a negative outcome or telling myself a negative story, I create distress equivalent to these events actually occurring.

I discovered something else. I discovered fear is never about something occurring in this moment. Fear is always about a possible *future* event. Fear is always about an event I imagine might happen. The cause of fear is amazingly simple. Fear occurs whenever I tell myself a negative story about a future event.

FEAR = Future + Negative Story

I'm similarly affected (but in the opposite way) whenever I tell myself a positive story about a future event. Imagine for a moment being on a holiday or some other pleasurable activity. Imagine all the wonderful things you will do on your holiday. What do you notice as you start to imagine these events? Almost immediately the emotions of joy, excitement and anticipation become activated.

Our imagination is very powerful. With the use of our imagination we are able to create pleasure or pain, joy or fear. Most people, however, use their imagination to create pain and fear. They do this by imagining negative outcomes rather than positive outcomes. Research shows that the average person thinks nine times as many negative thoughts as positive thoughts. This means they tell nine negative stories for every positive story. This explains why many people live in a chronic state of fear and anxiety.

> *I've had a very difficult life.*
> *Fortunately, most of it*
> *didn't happen.*

Mark Twain

The skill of negative imagining is not something we are born with. In fact humans have only two fears wired into their bodies at birth. Babies are instinctively uncomfortable with heights, and they become startled by loud noises. This is the extent of innate fear. This means all other fears are learned. It is my observation that creating fear through imagining negative outcomes is a skill that is highly encouraged in our culture. Let me offer an explanation.

A number of years ago I was an instructor at a local community college. One of the courses I taught was on personal wellness. Each new semester I would ask my students to bring a newspaper to class and a pair of scissors. The assignment was simple. Read the newspaper from beginning to end and clip out the articles. Place the negative and fear-based stories in one pile, and the positive and affirming stories in a second pile.

The results were always the same. The pile with the negative stories was considerable, often most of the newspaper. The positive stories made a much smaller pile, rarely more than a handful of articles. This phenomenon is true regardless of the medium – newspaper, television, or radio. The fact is we are inundated with a barrage of negative stories. Hearing, viewing, or reading negative stories has the same effect as imagining negative stories. They cause fear. They make us sick. They feed the negative wolf.

Most people fail to make the connection between their chronic anxiety and the near constant exposure to negative stories. This is because the constant presence of negativity makes it difficult for us to imagine life without it. There is a Native saying that captures this experience perfectly –

To the fish, the water is invisible.

In high school I participated in a biology experiment that is relevant to this discussion. In the experiment we placed a frog in boiling water. The frog immediately recognized the danger and jumped out. We then placed the frog in warm water. Slowly we heated the water to boiling. To our surprise the frog remained in the water and died.

Our instructor explained that the frog died because the gradual nature of the change prevented the frog from recognizing the danger. I think of this experiment when I observe our chronic exposure to negative stories. We are harmed by these negative stories, yet most of us fail to remove ourselves from this danger. Just as with the frog, the effect is fatal.

A number of years ago I read an article in a magazine for parents. The title of the article was, *Who Tells the Stories Your Children Hear?* In the article author Michael Warren explained that storytelling is one of the most powerful tools used to influence attitudes and behaviors.

He described how aboriginal cultures use storytelling as the primary means by which elders pass valuable information from one generation to the next. Embedded within the stories are the values, beliefs, and traditions important to the health and well-being of the individual and the community.

Warren then asked, *"Who tells the stories your*

children hear today?" For most the answer is obvious. Television has become the primary storyteller. Cartoons and comedy shows have replaced parents and grandparents in instructing our children with appropriate values and beliefs. This responsibility has been passed to a group of people we do not know, and whose values we may not share.

Not only do we allow others to be the primary storytellers to our children, we allow others to be our storyteller as well. We allow television, radio, newspapers and other media to define for us what is important and not important, what is good and bad, and what we should and should not value.

Given the power of story and the effect it has on our physical, mental, emotional, and spiritual bodies, it is essential we be more vigilant to the stories we tell ourselves and the stories we allow to be told to us if we desire to be happy, healthy and peaceful.

Imagining the worst feeds my Negative Wolf

*Sometimes the arrow
doesn't go where I intend.*
Native saying

2. Making a Mistake

Another way I fed my negative wolf was by thinking, *"I've made a mistake."* Most people believe they make mistakes. I discovered there is no such thing as a mistake.

Ray Woollam helped me to understand that there are no mistakes. Ray is an unusual thinker who has written a number of culture-challenging books including *Have a Plain Day* and *On Choosing with a Quiet Mind*.

I attended a seminar, which Ray facilitated. Ray began the seminar by asking, *"Who here has made a mistake?"* To no one's surprise everyone in the room raised their hand. Ray then invited us to share with the others the decision we considered the biggest mistake of our life. Ray wrote our answers on a large sheet of paper and posted the list at the front of the room.

In the group was a young woman by the name of Rebecca. When it was Rebecca's turn she announced her biggest mistake was, *"losing her virginity to a complete idiot."* The room erupted in laughter. Ray added to Rebecca's embarrassment by declaring that he liked her answer so much he intended to use it as the title of his next book! When the laughter subsided Ray invited Rebecca to share with the group how she lost her virginity.

Rebecca told us about a date with a man named Alan. She described the pleasure of his company while enjoying a delicious dinner at an expensive restaurant. After the meal she and Alan walked along the beach and shared stories. After several hours of talking and laughing Alan invited Rebecca to join him at his apartment. Rebecca accepted. While there, Alan and Rebecca made love.

Ray inquired whether Rebecca enjoyed herself that evening. The glow on Rebecca's face and the enthusiasm in her voice told everyone she had. Ray then asked if she made love to Alan by her own choosing. Rebecca affirmed that indeed it had been her decision. Ray then inquired, *"When did you discover Alan was a complete idiot?"* Rebecca replied, *"About six months later."* Ray then asked, *"At the time you made the decision to make love to Alan, did you think that it was a good decision?"*

"Yes," was Rebecca's answer.

This is the point Ray wanted us to appreciate. Whenever we make a decision, we choose the alternative that we think is the right one. Ray was even more emphatic. He declared we make the *best* decision available given the information, skill, and options available to us in that moment. No one *chooses* a mistake.

Ray then turned our attention to the list at the front of the room. He invited us to reflect on the decision we identified as the biggest mistake of our life. I thought about the decision to have my son immunized with a vaccine. For many years my wife and I regretted this decision and called it a mistake. Ray then asked, *"At the time you made the decision, did you think it was a good decision?"*

The answer from all of us was, *"Yes, of course. That's why we made the choice we did."*

I chose to have my son vaccinated because I thought it was what a responsible parent did, based on the information I knew at the time.

Ray then asked whether the concept of 'mistake' is universal – *Does everyone in the world think this way? Does everyone call these events mistakes?"* We all assumed everyone thought as we did. We couldn't imagine anyone not thinking this way.

Ray told us about giving a similar seminar to a group of First Nations people. He began the seminar just as he did ours, by asking the young aboriginal men and women to disclose their biggest mistake and listing their answers on a sheet of paper at the front of the room. Then Ray did something different. He asked the First Nation participants to contact a member of their community who spoke their traditional language. Their task was to identify the word for mistake in their own language.

When all the participants completed their assignment, Ray continued. He asked each of them to share the word for 'mistake' from their

Native language. Of the sixteen different tribes present, no one was able to identify a word for mistake. This is because the word 'mistake' and the idea it represents, does not exist in most aboriginal cultures.

The closest any of the Native tribes came to our Western concept of mistake was a tribe with a word that translated into the phrase: *"Sometimes when I place an arrow in my bow, the arrow doesn't go where I intend."* The word simply acknowledged that one doesn't always experience the outcome he or she anticipates. Absent was any notion of shame, blame, guilt, or embarrassment as is commonly associated with our use of the word mistake.

Sometime later a friend shared with me how the film and recording industry address this issue. In this industry mistakes are referred to as *'missed takes'*. They don't have the expectation that an actor or musician will perform perfectly every time. When a *'missed take'* occurs, they simply do another *'take'*.

Thomas Edison, the inventor of the electric light bulb, made approximately 1,400 mistakes before finally perfecting his invention. Rather than experience shame or guilt with each failure, Edison recognized each attempt moved him one step closer to his goal of creating a successful bulb.

From Ray's seminar I gained a new perspective. I came to understand that the word *'mistake'* is simply an idea, a concept, an intellectual construct, and not even a universally shared one at that. Don Miguel Ruiz, author of *The Four Agreements*, describes this as an *agreement*. He says we can choose to accept this agreement, or we can make another agreement.

When I reflected on my life and noticed where ideas and actions pointed me, I recognized that the idea – *"I made a mistake"* usually pointed me in the direction of anger, sadness, and shame.

I now accept that I make the best decisions possible given the information, skills, and options I possess in each moment. When I experience an outcome I do not anticipate, or when a '*missed take*' occurs, I simply do another take. I choose again.

The idea of making a mistake feeds my Negative Wolf.

A victim is someone who believes their past is more powerful than their present.

Eckhart Tolle

3. Thinking Like a Victim

In my journey I noticed something else about myself. I noticed I often made statements like:

> *I don't want to, but I have to.*
>
> *I don't want to get up, but I have to.*
>
> *I don't want to go to work, but I have to.*
>
> *I don't want to pay my taxes, but I have to.*
>
> *I don't want to diet, but I have to.*
>
> *I don't want to do this task, but I have to.*
>
> *I have no choice.*

When I made statements as these I felt angry, resentful, and powerless. These are the thoughts and feelings of someone who thinks of them self as a *victim*. I don't enjoy feeling like a victim. I don't like thinking that I have no choice. I don't want to be angry, frustrated, and resentful.

In examining this phenomenon I discovered that each of the above statements was not true.

The truth was I did want to get up. I did want to go to work. I did want to pay my taxes, diet, exercise, and all of the other things I did. I did these things because I preferred the consequences of doing them, rather than the consequences of not doing them.

I came to realize that I always have a choice. I always have a number of possibilities before me. I can choose to stay home, ignore my taxes, or eat whatever I want. Yet, while these choices are available to me, I behave in the ways I do because I trust these behaviors will bring me what I want now or in the future.

I discovered behavior is functional. All behavior serves a purpose. I work because of the benefits work provides me. I pay my taxes because I want the civic benefit my taxes make possible. I manage my diet because I want to be healthy and enjoy the many positive results thoughtful eating brings.

It is not about having to do anything. It's

Peace Begins With Me

about wanting the outcomes that these choices create.

In situations where something does happen not of my choosing (where the arrow doesn't go where I intend) I discovered that I can choose the *meaning* I assign to the event.

This discovery is one of the most powerful lessons I learned from my experience with my son. While I had no control over the fact my son was damaged by his vaccine shot, I did have control over the meaning I assigned to this outcome.

Initially the meaning I assigned was: *"This is awful."* and *"This is unacceptable."* The psychic was instrumental in helping me to assign a new meaning and acquire a new perspective with regards to my son's condition. In changing the meaning I assigned to this event, my *experience* of the event changed.

For much of my life I didn't know I could change the meaning that is assigned to an event. I assumed I had no choice but to accept the meanings I had been given by others. No choice but to think the way others thought. No choice but to feel anger and sadness at my son's condition. No choice but to feed the negative wolf.

Ray Woollam explained to me there is a serious epidemic in our world today; an epidemic he labels *"victimitis"*. By this he means that most people act as though they are a victim. A victim is someone who acts as though he or she has no choice. Victims are of the belief life happens *to* them. I agree with Woollam. I notice most people fail to embrace the power of choice. Most people think and act as if they are powerless.

We think and act like victims because this is what we are taught. We are regularly told we have no choice. To illustrate my point, take a moment to recall a recent newscast. If it were like most newscasts, you would have heard a politician or the CEO of a company declare how powerless he or she is. I regularly hear statements as: *"I had no choice but to raise taxes!"* or *"I had no choice but to lay off 400 employees."*

It's common for our leaders to want to convince us that what is happening is not of their choosing; that they are powerless to do otherwise. With this kind of modeling its not surprising that we too come to believe that we have no choice. It's not surprising that we learn to speak the language of victimitis: *"I don't want to, but I have to."*

I believe people are not being honest when they declare, *"I have no choice."* Rather, the truth is something like: *"I reviewed the options before me and because of what I value and the outcome I desire, I choose to raise taxes, lay off 400 employees, go to work, exercise, eat cheesecake, or whatever."*

I now know I'm not being honest when I say, *"I have no choice,"* or *"I don't want to but I have to."*

Thinking like a victim feeds my Negative Wolf

He is blessed who loses
no moment
of the passing life
in remembering the past.
Henry David Thoreau

Peace Begins With Me

4. Living in the Future or the Past

When I reflected on my life I noticed something very surprising. I noticed I spent very little time in the present. My attention was frequently focused on imagining the future or recalling the past. My mind was almost always somewhere other than where I was physically. I'd be sitting on a chair in my living room, yet my mind wasn't even in the room. It was imagining tomorrow's events or recalling events from previous days or years. I discovered my mind and body were rarely in the same place at the same time.

After I started paying attention to my thoughts, I noticed I felt a slight tension in my stomach whenever my mind was in a different place than where I was physically. I now believe this sensation is a message created by my body to inform me when I've become disconnected. By 'disconnected' I mean my mind and my body are not in the same place at the same time. I am no longer whole.

This experience can be explained using the metaphor of a home alarm system. By design the alarm system has a series of connections. These connections are between a door and the frame, or a window and the casing. If one of the connections is broken, an alarm immediately signals the disconnection. I notice this same phenomenon at work within me. My mind and body appear wired in such a way that whenever my mind and body become disconnected, an alarm goes off. I experience this alarm as the sensation of tension in my stomach. This tension is commonly experienced as anxiety.

I now accept that the experience of anxiety is important. It brings to my awareness the fact that I am not present, I am living either in the past or the future. Anxiety helps to remind me. That is, *re-mind* me.

Other experiences similar to anxiety serve this purpose as well. I notice a disturbance in my body when I'm driving my car and think I ought to be somewhere other than where I am – usually

Peace Begins With Me

farther along in the traffic! Road rage is the result of being disconnected. When I reconnect my mind with my body, my feeling of rage disappears.

I feel calm when my mind and body are in the same place at the same time. Author Eckhart Tolle introduced this notion of *presence* to me in his book, *The Power of Now*. Tolle states most people miss out on the present moment because they live either in the past or the future. Tolle invites us to notice where we spend our time. He very effectively captures the importance of living in the moment in this quote:

> *Most people live almost exclusively*
> *through memory or anticipation.*
> *Both are illusions.*
>
> *Unease, anxiety, tension, stress,*
> *worry, all forms of fear*
> *are caused by too much future*
> *and not enough presence.*

Guilt, regret, resentment, grievance,
sadness, bitterness,
and all forms of non-forgiveness
are caused by too much past
and not enough presence.

Many older people spend their life living in the past, in memory. Most young people live in the future, in anticipation. When we live mostly in the past or future we miss out on life in the now.

This moment is all we really have. It's all we ever have. The present is where life occurs. Until recently I spent very little time in the present moment. As a consequence I've missed much of my life.

Living primarily in the future or the past feeds my Negative Wolf.

5. Resisting Reality

Another lesson I learned during my journey with my son is that I spent much of my life resisting reality. I resist reality whenever I make statements such as:

> *It shouldn't be this way.*
>
> *It shouldn't be this cold.*
>
> *It should be sunnier today.*
>
> *I should be farther along in traffic.*
>
> *My team should have won the championship.*
>
> *That accident should never have happened.*
>
> *My boss shouldn't have done that.*
>
> *My partner should be more loving.*
>
> *I should have done better on that test.*
>
> *There should be no war.*

As you consider each of the statements listed

above, what do you notice? Do you notice that all of the statements are about something that has already occurred? The reality is: it *is* cold. It *is* cloudy. I'm *not* farther along in the traffic. My favorite team did *not* win the championship. The accident *did* happen. We *are* at war.

Each of the original statements resists something that already exists.

For years I told myself, *"My son shouldn't have been damaged by the vaccine shot."* Whenever I made this statement, I felt angry, sad, and full of resentment.

Most people, myself included, seem to be of the opinion that the act of resisting will change whatever it is we are resisting.

I finally recognized any resistance is futile. The act of resisting doesn't change the object of my resistance. It does, however, change *me*.

It changes me into someone who is angry, frustrated and resentful. No amount of *should-ing* or *would-having* will change something that already exists.

Resisting reality is another way of feeding my negative wolf. Resisting doesn't create change. It does not move me closer to my goal. It points me in a direction other than where I wish to go.

When I ask myself: *"Does it work? Does resisting point me in the direction I wish to go?"* The clear answer is *"No"*.

Resisting reality feeds my Negative Wolf

Forgiveness is giving up all hope
of a better past.
Anonymous

Peace Begins With Me

6. Delaying Happiness

I often heard myself saying: *"I'll be happy when . . .*

> *. . . . . the weekend comes."*

> *. . . . . I get a job."*

> *. . . . . I'm on holidays."*

> *. . . . . I retire. "*

> *. . . . . I get married."*

> *. . . . . I get divorced."*

> *. . . . . I have children."*

> *. . . . . the children leave home."*

> *. . . . . the mortgage is paid off."*

> *. . . . . I win the lottery."*

When I make statements such as these, I'm saying, *"I'm not happy now,"* and *"I'll be happy some time in the future."* I've discovered that this way of thinking doesn't serve me. It doesn't increase my happiness. Instead, it delays my happiness. It convinces me I need something other than what I have in order to be happy. It removes happiness from my present and places it somewhere in my future.

For many years I told myself, *"I'll be happy when my son stops seizing."* All the while, as he continued to seize, I felt angry, sad and depressed. If I experienced any happiness, it vanished as soon as my son started seizing again. Because my son's medical condition was outside of my control, my happiness was outside of my control.

Even on those occasions when some items on my list finally occurred, I noticed my happiness was short lived. A new item would always replace the now acquired item. I now understand that my unhappiness was due to my *thinking* rather than an absence of items or events.

When I acted as though my happiness was something to be acquired in the future, I failed to experience happiness. It continued to elude me.

I now accept that my happiness is not dependent upon acquiring things or events. It's not about the job, retirement, getting married, getting divorced, winning the lottery, or my son's health. It's a fallacy to think happiness comes from things or events.

This way of thinking reminds me of a cartoon from my childhood. In the cartoon a donkey strains to reach a carrot that has been suspended in front of him. The donkey's owner cleverly placed the carrot just beyond the donkey's reach in order to keep the donkey moving. I now see how I have lived most of my life like the donkey. I lived as though my happiness was just beyond my reach.

Upon reflection it is not surprising that we think this way. We are inundated with hundreds, if not thousands, of commercials every day. Virtually every advertisement and commercial is purposely designed to convince us we will be happy when we acquire the product or service that the ad is promoting. The advertisement promises happiness in our future.

Unfortunately, 'in the future' is exactly where it stays.

This phenomenon isn't exclusive to happiness. The same principle holds true with other experiences. I also used to believe:

> *I'll be peaceful when . . .*
>
> *I'll be joyful when . . .*
>
> *I'll be content when . . .*
>
> *I'll be loving when . . .*
>
> *I'll be loved when . . .*
>
> *I'll be good enough when . . .*

Recently I became aware I was telling myself, *"I'll be generous when . . ."* I imagined at some point in my life being wealthy enough to share my prosperity with others. It finally occurred to me that my intention to be generous was always located in the future. With this awareness, I decided it was possible for me to be generous now with the resources I have in this moment. Continually projecting my generosity into the future didn't serve me, and it certainly didn't serve others.

Regularly I hear people make statements as, *"I'll be attractive when I lose weight"*, *"I'll be lovable when I get a job, complete my counseling"*, or other similar statements. This way of thinking means happiness, joy, love and peace will remain elusive.

Delaying Happiness feeds my Negative Wolf

What Do You Notice?

Do you see yourself in any of these examples? Do you recognize some of the ways that you are feeding your negative wolf? Which ways of thinking and acting do you commonly engage in?

What do you notice is the impact of thinking and behaving in these ways? What direction do they point you in? Which wolf do you feed?

I regularly observe clients, friends, family and myself feeding the negative wolf. Consistent with each of these ways of thinking are the feelings of distress, anger, sadness and resentment.

If your goal is to experience more peace, joy, and happiness, it is important to understand how you are feeding your negative wolf.

Learn to recognize the actions and ideas that point you in the direction of anger, sadness and despair.

*You can't create a solution
with the same mindset
that created the problem.*

Albert Einstein

The best way to predict the future
is to create it.

Peace Begins With Me

Chapter Four

Feeding the Positive Wolf

I've discovered it is possible to think and act in new ways. It is possible to change the direction I'm headed. It is possible to increase my experience of peace, joy and happiness. It is possible to feed the positive wolf.

Being peaceful, joyful, and happy does not depend on being good enough, smart enough, or deserving enough. Nor does it require unique or special circumstances. The ability to experience greater peace and joy has to do with knowing how. I believe our society has done an inadequate job in educating people how to be in a state of peace. Many of our cultural institutions are more accomplished at teaching fear than trust, in promoting judgment than acceptance, and in encouraging negative thinking rather than positive thinking. I believe that most people simply don't know how to be happy, peaceful, and joyful.

At the same time one of my core beliefs is every person does the best they can with what they know. I like to use the analogy of a toolbox when describing this idea. I call our skills and knowledge "tools", and the combined wisdom and learning gained over a lifetime, our "toolbox". We are born with an empty toolbox. Some individuals are fortunate to have wise teachers and rich life experiences that contribute to the filling of their toolbox. Others are less fortunate and their toolbox remains largely empty.

I believe the inability to achieve peace, joy, and happiness is due to a lack of tools. Therefore, the remainder of this book is dedicated to describing the tools that I discovered pointed me in the direction of peace, joy and happiness. I share my tools with you so you may add them to your toolbox. In my experience, the more tools you have, the greater your success in life.

Three Common Responses

When sharing the material in this book with others, most people respond in one of three ways. Many people are excited by the ideas and eager to explore the difference they could make in their life. Others are quick to inform me there is nothing new in what I offer – they have heard it all before. Finally, there are some individuals who respond with, *"Ted, it seems you're from a different planet. Maybe you ought to go back to where you came from!"* I have come to appreciate each of the responses!

In truth, there is little new in the material I present here. All of these messages described here have been said before. Some of the concepts have indeed been known for thousands of years.

Unfortunately, most of these ideas have long since been forgotten or discarded, judged as either too simplistic or unscientific. My intention in writing this book is to remind you of this valuable ancient knowledge, and present it in a way that makes it more relevant for living in today's world.

Earlier I referenced the work of Don Miguel Ruiz, author of the book *The Four Agreements*. Ruiz states that we enter into *agreements* with others. Agreements that define what is considered important, not important, and how the world works.

The problem, according to Ruiz, is many of the agreements that we have accepted are no longer true or valid. He encourages us to reflect upon our agreements and, if necessary, develop new agreements.

What I offer in the pages that follow might simply be considered other agreements about how the world works. Through my own experience I came to recognize new and different agreements to assist me with managing and enjoying my life.

For those of you who are challenged by the ideas that follow, I have one request – when considering the material in this book, please refrain from attempting to judge whether the ideas or suggestions are "*right*" or "*wrong*". Most people have a tendency to want to do this. Instead, I invite you to use a different criterion to assess the merit of the ideas presented here.

I invite you to evaluate the ideas based on the following questions:

- *Would this work?*
- *Would this idea or strategy increase my peace, joy, and happiness?*
- *Which direction does this point me in?*
- *Which wolf does it feed?*

I believe the *rightness* of an idea is dependent on the degree to which it works. As a family therapist with more than 20 years' experience in providing individual, relationship, and family therapy, I'm regularly asked, *"What is the right answer?"*

As a way of responding, I typically do three things.

First I ask, *"Is what you are doing now working?"* Most often the answer is *no.* I explain the right answer must then be some other action.

Next, I help them generate a list of possible solutions to address their challenges.

Finally, I encourage them to experiment with these potential solutions until they find one that works.

The right answer is the one that works!

I believe life's ultimate question is: *"Does this work?"* Unfortunately, most people have been taught to ask: *"Is this right?"*

I've noticed that when the focus is on judging the *rightness* or *wrongness* of something, we often fail to notice whether the action works.

*Out beyond the ideas of wrong doing
and right doing there is a field.
I'll meet you there.*

Rumi

Many people struggle when confronted with new ideas. Author Lee Johnson describes this struggle in his best selling book *How to Escape Your Comfort Zones.* I believe that the struggle occurs because the new idea is unfamiliar and often runs counter to one they currently hold. While it is easier and more comfortable to stay with old and familiar ways of thinking, this prevents change. Change requires being willing to let go of what is known and familiar, and embrace the mysterious and the unfamiliar. It demands that we be willing to become uncomfortable.

In my efforts to encourage others to consider new ideas, I share the following folk wisdom:

If you want comfort,
find people who agree with you.

If you want growth,
find people who disagree with you.

Disagreement offers great potential for growth. In disagreement exists the opportunity to expand one's present knowledge and see the world from a larger perspective, a perspective that includes another way of thinking.

My hope is that the ideas contained in this book will cause you some genuine discomfort, and in so doing, offer possibilities for growth.

I offer a few final thoughts for your consideration as you venture into the realm of new ideas. These comments speak to the importance of doing something different if you wish to be successful in life.

I refer to them as Principles of Success.

Principles of Success

*If you want something
you've never had before,
you must be willing to do something
you've never done before.*

*Insanity is doing the same thing
and expecting a different outcome.*

If we desire an outcome different from what we are currently experiencing, then we must do something different from what we are doing. More of the same activity can only produce the same results. Or, said yet another way,

If nothing changes, nothing changes.

If you are interested in change because you desire more peace, joy, and happiness, then it is imperative you do something other than what you are already doing. My intention is to offer you a variety of ideas and tools to assist you in doing something different.

As you read the following chapter I encourage you to identify those tools you are willing to play with, ideas you want to explore further, and strategies you commit to experimenting with. Pay particular attention to any idea or strategy that seems strange or unusual.

It is often the strangest ideas that offer the greatest potential for growth. This is because they introduce you to something completely new and different, and have the potential to change your direction.

The following is a list of tools that I discovered fed my positive wolf. At the end of this book I will invite you to similarly identify three tools you commit to using in your own life in the upcoming week.

Ways to Feed Your Positive Wolf

1. Take responsibility for assigning meaning

2. Use your imagination creatively

3. Live in the present

4. Choose what does the most good

5. Accept Reality

6. Trust

7. Pay attention to your pain

8. Schedule worry time

9. Be happy now

10. Breathe from your diaphragm

*We are disturbed
not by what happens to us,
but by our thoughts
about what happens.*

Epictetus - Greek Philosopher

Peace Begins With Me

Tool #1 – Take Responsibility for Assigning Meaning

One of the most important ideas I discovered during my journey with my son is the importance of taking responsibility for the *meaning* I assign to the events in my life. The significance of this first became evident as I explored the cause of the stress in my life. My exploration led me to understand that there is a difference between *stress* and *distress*.

While many people use these two words interchangeably, they actually represent very different concepts. Medical researcher Hans Selye was the first to articulate the distinction in the 1970s with his work – *Stress without Distress.* Understanding the difference between stress and distress increases your capacity to create more peace and joy.

So, what *is* the difference between stress and distress? If you were to speak with a civil engineer who is responsible for designing a bridge, he might describe stress as a *force, pressure, or weight* that must be considered to ensure the bridge will withstand many different conditions. He would explain that the source of the stress is located in the external world.

If we use the engineer's definition of stress and apply it to our life, then we might say stress is an *external force, pressure, or weight exerted upon us.* If we agree that this is the definition of stress, then what is *distress*? I've discovered distress is an *internal* force. Distress is my *response* to stress; my response to the forces, pressures, or weight of life. Distress is created in my mind by the *meaning* I assign to stress.

In life we experience many different events. All of them create some level of stress. In and of themselves, these events are neither good nor bad, they simply *are*. Most people, however, don't experience life's events as neutral. Instead, we insist on labeling events. The act of labeling involves assigning meaning.

Depending on the meaning or label we assign,

Peace Begins With Me

we can have a completely different experience of an event. It's entirely possible to experience both joy and anger from the same event.

Event *(stress)*	Meaning A	:	Joy
	Meaning B	:	Laughter
	Mcaning C	:	Anger
	Meaning D	:	Distress

Let me demonstrate this concept with a simple example. I play a round of golf and finish with a score of 80. What experience will I have from this achievement? The answer is, *"It depends"*. It depends on the meaning I assign to my score.

The meaning I assign will be influenced by the kind of a golfer I am, and my expectations. If I usually score in the 90s, a score of 80 is likely to result in absolute delight! I might be inspired to celebrate my success by buying drinks for everyone after the game. But if I normally shoot in the low 70s, a score of 80 is likely to cause disappointment and frustration. I might even decide this game is not for me.

In both examples the score is exactly the same. Yet, in one situation I feel joyful and generous, while in the other I feel disappointed and frustrated.

The critical point here is that my experience is not dependent upon the *external* event – the score – but, rather, my experience is dependent upon *the meaning I assign* to my score, an *internal* event. The meaning I assign determines my experience.

> *Between stimulus and response*
> *is the greatest power -*
> *the freedom to choose.*
>
> Stephen Covey

The reason the distinction between stress and distress is important, is because one of these conditions is within my control (*distress*), while the other is outside of my control (*stress*). When I use these two terms interchangeably, I combine something that I have power over, with something I don't. The result is confusion and powerlessness. Understanding the distinction allows me to focus my actions on those things I can control, and release those things outside of my control.

For many years I believed my unhappiness was caused by the *events* in my life. While I held this belief I felt powerless to alleviate my unhappiness because most events were outside of my control. My son's medical condition is an example of this. Now I understand that my unhappiness, anger, and other forms of distress, were a result of the *meaning* I assigned to events. These emotional experiences were *my* creation. I created them by the kind of thoughts I had.

Quite simply, distress is a consequence of the meaning we assign to the events in our life. It is the meaning, not the events, which determine our experiences.

If I fully accept this idea, then the experience of *distress* is within my power. By taking responsibility for the meaning I assign, I can eliminate anger, frustration, and other forms of distress – regardless of the stress. I can, in Selye's words, have "*stress without distress*". If this sounds too good to be true, read the following story:

The Best Day of My Life

Jerome is friend of mine. When Jerome was twenty years old, he and a group of friends decided to go water skiing. Unfortunately, they decided to do so while under the influence of mind-altering substances. Jerome was on skis while his friend drove the boat. Because his friend was intoxicated, he steered the boat too close to the shore. Jerome ran into large rocks located there. The collision broke Jerome's back, severing his spinal cord and permanently paralyzing him below his chest.

A few years ago I witnessed Jerome speaking to a group of adolescents in the gymnasium of a local high school. During his presentation one of the student remarked to Jerome, *"The day you broke your back must have been the worst day of your life."* Jerome surprised the youth by replying, *"No, the day of my accident was actually the best day of my life."*

The confused youth asked, *"How could that be? You're paralyzed and need to use a wheel chair!"*

Jerome explained: *"Up until that day I spent most of my life either stoned or drunk. I didn't care about anybody or anything. All I cared about was where my next joint was coming from or the next case of beer. When I broke my back I was taken to hospital. I spent the next two years recovering and learning to live in a wheel chair. I had lots of time to think.*

One of the questions I thought about often was "What will I do with my life now?" After much consideration I decided to return to college and become a drug and alcohol counselor working with youth. And that is what I did. Now I have the good fortune of working with people I enjoy and I do something impor-

tant. Because of my experience I make a difference in the lives of the young people I meet.

As far as I'm concerned, the day I broke my back is the day I woke up. It's the day I was born. It's the day my life began to have purpose and meaning. That is why it's the best day of my life."

Each of us knows or has heard of someone in a difficult life situation similar to Jerome's. It's possible to imagine this person spending the rest of his life feeling angry and resentful, possibly even suicidal. Yet Jerome labels this day the best day of his life. Jerome's story taught me it is not *events* that determine my happiness or sadness; rather it's the *meaning* I assign to these events.

From A Canadian Perspective

It is time to lighten things up with a Canadian joke.

A few years ago a number of Canadians were in a car accident and died. Because these individuals were bad people they went straight to Hell.

When people first arrive in Hell, the Devil checks to make sure they are sufficiently miserable. So, shortly after the Canadians arrived, the Devil stopped by for a visit. He noticed that the new arrivals were pretty delighted with their new surroundings. Curious about their happiness, the Devil asked the reason. They replied, *"We're from Canada. It's cold there. It's warm here."*

Because it would damage his reputation if people enjoyed their time in Hell, the Devil urgently needed to do something about the situation. His solution was to turn the heat up even more. When the Devil returned the next day, he found the Canadians dressed in shorts and lounging on deck chairs. The Devil was furious. He demanded to know the reason for their continued good spirits. They replied, *"We're just beginning to thaw out."*

The Devil realized something was terribly wrong. Somehow, the intense heat didn't work on these Canadians. He had to try something different. He thought for a long while, and then decided to make Hell freezing cold. He was confident the extreme cold would do the trick.

When the Devil looked in on the Canadians on the third day he discovered they were having a party. They were laughing, dancing, and hugging one another. The Devil demanded, *"What is going on here?"* The Canadians replied, *"We're fans of the Toronto Maple Leafs. They haven't won a championship in decades. We figure they must have finally won, because Hell has frozen over!"*

The moral to this story is that it's the meaning we assign to the events in our life, rather than the events themselves, that creates peace and joy. William Shakespeare said it this way:

> *There is nothing either good or bad,*
> *but thinking makes it so.*

This first tool is about taking responsibility for

the meaning we assign to events. In doing so, we access the power to create more peace and joy. By thoughtfully choosing the meaning we assign, we are able to determine our experience in life.

These days, when I experience anger, sadness or disappointment, I accept that I've created this experience by the meaning I've assigned. As soon as I realize this, I change the meaning and thus my experience.

The visit to the psychic was instrumental in helping me to understand the power of meaning. The psychic's words had no power over the events in my life. My son continued to seize with the same frequency after my visit as before. However, by thinking of my son as a teacher my experience of him changed. Where once I felt only anger, frustration, and sadness, I now experience joy, beauty, and gratitude in my relationship with my son.

Taking responsibility for the Meaning I assign to life's events feeds my Positive Wolf

Imagination is more important than knowledge.

Albert Einstein

Tool #2 – Use your imagination creatively

The next tool for your consideration involves the use of your imagination. Our imagination is very powerful. Our imagination is the mechanism that enables us to create. There is an expression that says, *"All things are created twice – first in someone's mind, then in physical form"*.

I've noticed that creative people share one thing in common. They *see* their creation before they begin. The painter sees the completed painting on the blank canvas. The sculptor sees her finished carving in the untouched block of wood. The musician knows what the music will sound like before the score is written. Creation happens by first *seeing* in your mind's eye what it is you intend to create.

This strategy of seeing before beginning exists in other sectors of society as well. Professional athletes describe how they see the outcome of their actions before they begin. Stories about golfers regularly describe how they see the shot before they hit the ball. Olympic athletes are taught to visualize their dive, run, performance, or routine over and over again in their mind. They do this because imagining the outcome they desire contributes to their success.

Even though it happened several years ago, I remember a celebration I watched of a football team that had just won a championship. The memory stayed with me because of the intriguing response by one of the players. His team, the team that won, was the underdog in the match and the odds of their winning were extremely low.

During the post-game program the interviewer asked many of the winning players, *"Did you expect to win?"* This player replied, *"Of course we expected to win. During training camp, our coach had us place paper bands on our ring finger and imagine we were wearing the championship ring."*

Many medical practitioners also recognize the power of the imagination. Dr. Carl Simonton, a renowned cancer oncologist, uses the power of the imagination to heal his patients. Borrowing an image from a popular video game, Dr. Simonton taught his patients to imagine their cancer cells being eaten by a giant PAC MAN. His research confirmed that patients who practice positive imagining as part of their treatment have significantly better rates of recovery than patients who don't.

Dr. Bernie Segal, another oncologist and author of the book, *"Love, Medicine, and Miracles"* discovered exactly the same phenomenon when he researched exceptional cancer patients. Curious about patients who outlived their terminal diagnosis, Segal discovered the secret of these exceptional patients was their positive imagination.

Imagining the outcome one desires occurs in the corporate sector as well. Every successful business develops a picture of the financial status desired at the end of the fiscal year. This imagining is known as a budget, a financial projection, or a strategic plan. Business owners do this because they recognize that this process contributes to their success.

In 1952 Yale University conducted a study in its business school. The graduating class was asked, *"Who has a written goal plan for his or her life?"* Only three percent responded affirmatively.

Twenty years later the same group was re-interviewed. The three percent who had written out their life plan were profoundly more successful than the remaining ninety-seven percent who had not. Their study confirmed that visioning contributes to success.

Greased Ball Bearings

The following is a simple exercise to allow you to experience the power of your imagination.

Stand up and extend your arms straight out from your sides. While extending your arms and keeping your feet planted firmly on the ground, rotate your waist. Rotate as far as you can and hold yourself there. With your eyes, follow the length of one of your extended arms beyond your fingertips to a place on the wall to mark the extent of your rotation. Remember this spot. Rotate a few more times to be certain this spot marks the furthest rotation possible.

Now, drop your arms and close your eyes. Imagine your waist has been suddenly transformed into ball bearings. Imagine that these ball bearings are well greased to allow you to rotate easily. Even imagine feeling the slipperiness of the grease inside your waist.

Continue to keep your eyes closed. Now imagine that you are able to rotate easily because of the ball bearings in your waist. See in your imagination the spot on the wall that indicated the farthest extent of your previous rotation. Imagine approaching this spot and being able to move past it. Imagine another spot farther on the wall that marks your additional rotation. When you have fixed this new spot in your mind, open your eyes.

Now complete the exercise. Extend your arms and rotate as far as you possibly can. Mark the spot. Close your eyes and use your imagination as described above. Then open your eyes and rotate as far as you can. Everyone who tries this exercise is able to rotate farther the second time. This is because of the power of your imagination.

Intention and Attention

If you wish to create something, two actions are required – ***intention*** and **attention**. *Intention* means being able to answer the question, *"What do I intend?"* or *"What does success look like?"* It means having clearly identified the outcome desired before one begins.

The action of *attention* involves the focusing of awareness. *"What am I attending to? What am I focusing on? What am I looking at?"*

A focused attention is critical to achieving the outcome one desires.

*Conscious change is brought about
by two qualities:
attention and intention.
Attention energizes.
Intention transforms.*

Deepak Chopra

Often when I present this strategy I'm told this idea is "new age" thinking. In truth, it is "old age" thinking. The act of imagining the outcome one desires is an idea that has been around for thousands of years. Most readers are aware of the Dead Sea Scrolls discovered in the 1950's in the Middle East. These scrolls have since been translated to disclose their contents.

In one of the scrolls the question is asked, *"How do miracles happen?"* The answer contained in the ancient scroll is, *"If you want to create a mir-*

acle, two actions are required. The first action is to see in your mind's eye what you want to create. The second action is to feel what it would feel like to have this event occur. When you combine the seeing and the feeling, miracles happen."

This is my experience also. I've discovered my imagination is very powerful. The following is a story of when I used my imagination to create something I desired.

One Friday evening one of our family's cars broke down. It was an old car and not worth repairing. We urgently needed to replace the vehicle to manage our day-to-day affairs.

That evening I sat in silence and imagined the kind of vehicle I desired. I imagined a vehicle with four doors to easily accommodate my two young children. I decided I wanted something reliable and so imagined an import vehicle with the reputation of being well designed and trustworthy. I then looked at the balance in my savings account and decided I was willing to spend a maximum of $1,000 on the purchase. Finally, I imagined the joy I would feel in having a vehicle that met these conditions.

The next morning I placed my son in his wheelchair and began walking in the lane behind my home. A few minutes later a neighbor noticed the two of us and called out to me. He asked if I knew of anyone who was looking to buy a car. I told him I was intending to purchase a car that very weekend.

He proceeded to show me the car that he was selling. He explained that his parents celebrated their 25th wedding anniversary the previous evening. He and his siblings had purchased a new car for them as a gift and he was selling their old vehicle.

The car was an 18-year-old Toyota Corolla. It was in excellent condition in spite of its advanced age. My neighbor said his parents purchased the car new and took very good care of it. I noticed the car was a four-door vehicle. When I asked how much he wanted for the car, my neighbor told me he placed an ad in the local paper listing the price at $1,200. He admitted, however, that he would be satisfied with receiving $1,000 for the car. I had my car within 30 minutes of being awake that morning.

Some people who hear this story respond, *"It's a nice story Ted. . . but the world doesn't work that way."*

My question is, *What if it does? What if our world **does** work this way? What if our life is created by the action of our imagination?*

If this is true, then most people are in serious trouble. This is because most people use their imagination negatively. Most imagine the outcomes they *don't* want, rather than the outcomes they *do* want.

I remind you of information I shared earlier, that the average person thinks nine times as many negative thoughts as positive thoughts. If we accept the possibility that our imagination is powerful in creating outcomes, then we need to be more vigilant with how we use our imagination.

The other tool of creation is *attention*. This means noticing where you focus your awareness. I discovered that attention is equally important. We have all heard the phrase: *"Is the glass half full, or half empty?"* In my journey I came to understand the glass is both half full *and* half empty. Both conditions exist at the same time.

And when I focus my attention on the full part, I have a different experience than when I focus my attention on the empty part. Let me give you an example.

During the first four years of my son's life I focused all my attention on the parts of Joshua that were 'empty'. All I could see were his disabilities. All I noticed were the things my son couldn't do and how different he was from the other children. Whenever I focused my attention on my son's disabled parts I felt anger, sadness and resentment.

As I matured in my thinking I learned to focus my attention on the 'full' parts of my son. I began to notice his smile, his touch, and his enthusiasm for the simple things in life. When I focused my attention on his full parts I felt joy, happiness and love.

Several years ago when Josh entered grade seven, he was fortunate to have a teacher who saw his full parts. The following is a true story that captures the power of attention.

The Toss of A Coin

It was a hot August day when two teachers, Mike and Jeff, sat in the shade of a maple tree to assign students to their respective classes. These were no ordinary teachers. Rivaling their love of teaching was their love of sport. Both were active in all kinds of athletic endeavors. Following a time-honored sporting tradition, the toss of a coin would be used to decide who got first pick. Like captains of a team, Mike and Jeff decided to alternate picks until all 70 students had been assigned to a class.

With mock seriousness Mike held the coin firmly in his grasp and nodded to Jeff. When Jeff acknowledged he was ready, Mike flipped the coin end-over-end. At its peak Jeff called *"Heads"*. With the precision of someone having excellent hand-eye coordination, Mike grabbed the coin and slapped it onto the back of his wrist. Both waited impatiently as if something of extreme importance depended on the outcome. Little did they know how important this decision would become.

As Mike removed his hand from atop the coin, Jeff yelled with exuberance: *"Heads! I get first pick!"* Despite Mike grumbling, *"Best of 2 out of 3. . ."* Jeff began reviewing the names on the list. After seemingly endless deliberation, Jeff's eyes rested on the name – Joshua Kuntz.

Josh was not your typical student. Because of his seizure disorder, Josh's intellectual capacity had been reduced to the level of a two year old. His language was the most affected. He could speak only a few dozen words, and even these with difficulty. An unfamiliar listener would need someone to translate Josh's words. Also, the uncontrolled nature of his seizure disorder meant Josh could convulse at any moment. Having Josh as a student would mean constant vigilance to ensure his safety and assistance with every aspect of his day. And yet, Jeff's eyes stayed focused on Josh's name. Eventually Jeff announced his first choice: *"I choose Josh."*

Mike was a relatively new teacher to the school and did not know every student on the list – but Mike knew Josh. Josh was hard to miss in the school. He knew Josh was a child with significant challenges – both intellectual and medical. *"I don't understand,"* Mike said, *"Why would you choose a child with disabilities with your first pick?"*

I'm told Jeff smiled at Mike's question. It was not an unusual question since most people who meet Josh for the first time see only the disabled parts. Jeff knew it took time to see beyond Josh's disabilities and acknowledge the parts of him that are delightful and beautiful.

Jeff responded this way, *"Mike, I have been around the school for a number of years. I couldn't help but notice Josh. But more than that I noticed how the other children responded to Josh.*

"I noticed they were eager to greet him when they passed him in the hallways. I noticed the children would rush to complete an assignment to earn the opportunity to read to him while the others finished.

"I noticed boys and girls alike wanted to hold his hand as he was being pushed down the hallway in his chair. I noticed children modifying games to include him. I noticed students gently comforting him after a seizure.

"What I noticed is the children are kinder and more gentle when in Josh's presence. I think having Joshua in my class will make it a kinder and gentler place for everyone."

A wonderful thing happened under the shade of the maple tree that summer. A young child whom many saw only as disabled was acknowledged for his gifts. And what was his gift? By way of his disability, Josh creates opportunities for others to express their humanity. Anyone who visited that grade seven class that year noticed something different. They may not have known that the toss of a coin and the selection of a young student with disabilities was responsible, but the spirit of caring and compassion in the room was unmistakable.

I'm grateful Josh had Jeff as his teacher. Josh's life was enriched because Jeff focused his attention on Joshua's gifts and contributions rather than his deficits. Jeff also taught me to attend to my son in this way.

Other Examples of Attention

I witnessed the power of attention while working in a treatment center for young children with severe behavioral challenges. The program's treatment strategy was simple. When a child was admitted to the program, a label was pinned onto his or her clothing. Written on the label was the following message, *"Catch me doing good."*

The unusual message served as a reminder to the staff to pay attention to the child's positive behaviors rather than their negative behaviors. I was amazed at how quickly the children's behavior improved when attention was consistently focused on their positive behaviors.

A member of the pit crew with a professional auto racing team told me a story that is another example of the power of attention. He explained the strategy racecar drivers use to help prevent them from crashing into the barriers that surround a racetrack.

He explained, *"In the event the driver loses control and the car starts heading toward a barrier, the driver does not look at the barrier. Instead, he focuses all of his attention on an opening in the field of cars.*

"By focusing on an opening, the car moves in that direction. Should the driver focus on the barrier, he will crash into it every time."

I often use the lesson from the racecar driver in my daily life. When things feel out of control and it looks as though I am heading for a crash, I remind myself to look for the openings. I place my attention on the outcomes I desire rather than on the barriers.

> *Obstacles are what you notice*
> *when you take your eyes*
> *off the goal.*

In my counselling practice I regularly use the tools of attention and intention to help my clients create more success in their lives. When working with couples who are in a relationship crisis I intentionally change the focus of their attention.

Often they arrive ready to share with me all the things that are wrong in their relationship. Rather than listen to their list of complaints, I invite the couple to have a different conversation. I ask each of them to describe what a successful relationship looks and feels like from their perspective. The therapy becomes extremely powerful when the focus shifts from what isn't working, to what a successful relationship might look like.

Creating the kind of life one wishes is a wonderful way to live. Yet most people *react* to life rather than intentionally *create* their life.

Neale Donald Walsch, author of *Conversations With God,* shares a helpful reminder that is built into the words REACTION and CREATION. He asks, *"When you examine these two words, what do you notice?"*

The simple answer is that the letter "C" is located in a different position. In the word *reaction* the "C" is embedded in the middle of the word. In the word *creation,* the "C" is the first letter.

His message is, in order to create something you need to "C" (see) first.

Living with Intention and Attention

This tool makes use of your imagination to see the outcomes you want to create, and then keeping your focus on these outcomes. Common expressions that capture this message are:

Look where you want to go.
Keep the end in mind.
Keep your eye on the ball.
You can't hit a target you can't see.

I am sure these expressions are familiar to you. The challenge is to consistently apply this philosophy to daily life. Many people use their imagination to create wonderful works of art, crafts, and food dishes, even parking spots at the local mall. I am inviting you to use your imagination in even more powerful ways – to consciously use the power of intention and attention to create what you desire in life.

Begin each day with intention. Ask yourself,

"What do I intend for this day? What outcomes do I desire? What do I want to experience?" Begin business or family meetings with declared intention. Take a moment before making a phone call or writing an email to identify your desired outcome. Be clear with yourself what a successful meeting, conversation, or action would accomplish.

Be conscious about where you place your attention. When events occur other than what you intended, focus on the openings. Look for the possibilities.

Finally, at the end of your day, make a gratitude list by acknowledging the parts of your day you are grateful for. This keeps your focus positive.

Using my imagination Positively feeds my Positive Wolf

Live each moment completely,
and the future will take care of itself.
Fully enjoy the wonder and beauty
of each instant.

Parmahansa Yogananda

Tool #3 – Live in the Present

In a previous chapter I explained what happens when your mind and your body are in two places at the same time – you experience the alarm of anxiety, and you feel disconnected. This sense of disconnection is common. Most people live somewhere other than in the present. Elderly people frequently live in the past by focusing their attention on what they remember. Their preoccupation is with: *"I remember when . . ."*

Young people tend to live in the future thinking: *"I can hardly wait until . . ."* The result is that most people are rarely fully present. Their mind and body are disconnected – one part here, the other there. Being disconnected from the present robs us of the beauty, joy, and peace available in this moment.

Author Eckhart Tolle is the individual who brought the idea of presence to my awareness. Until my exposure to his message in *The Power of Now,* I was often somewhere else. Usually I was months, even years ahead of myself. In addition, I regularly told myself negative stories about my future. Now that I am aware of the effect of negative imagining, I understand the reason I was in pain so much of the time.

From my explorations I came to the realization that the present moment is *always* manageable. I am always able to manage whatever shows up *in this moment*.

What is not manageable are my negative thoughts and imagining about the future, about what might happen, or my remembering of the past. This is because the future and the past don't exist. They are illusions. I cannot change what doesn't exist. The now is all I have. The now is all I'll ever have.

When I live in the present, I experience an inner peace. Both my mind and my body become quiet. There is stillness within. I am safe in this moment. When I am present, fear does not exist. Nor does anger, resentment, grief, guilt, or worry.

Life is simple. I simply notice, and then choose.

What stops us from living in the moment? Living in the moment takes courage. It takes courage to trust that we can manage without anticipating every possible danger or problem. Many of us think if we didn't anticipate every possible danger and take steps to prevent it, we could not survive. Because of this belief, most people spend the majority of their life living in their imagined future.

In addition, they are constantly imagining negative outcomes, which create a chronic state of fear. When we imagine a negative future, we experience a double blow. We live in fear, and the present moment eludes us. We can't focus on the future and live in the present at the same time.

As I experimented with living in the present, I discovered a depth of peace and joy I had never known before. I enjoy my life more when I am in the now. My experience of peace is richer and deeper when I am present.

If your goal is to experience greater peace, joy, and happiness, I invite you to experiment with living in the present.

One way to do this is to simply notice where you are. *Are you living in the past, the present, or the future?* If you notice you are somewhere other than the present, return your attention to this moment. Simply asking the question, *"Where am I?"* brings you into present moment awareness.

Get Back to Your Senses

One of the tools that enabled me to become more present is called, *'Get Back to Your Senses'*. I acquired this tool while attending a weekend silent retreat. At the start of the retreat the participants were asked to complete a number of tasks including: feeling the bark of a tree, smelling the fragrance of a flower, listening to the sound of running water, feeling the morning dew on the grass, studying the design of a leaf, and tasting the salt of the ocean. I asked our facilitator the reason he wanted us to complete these activities. He explained the purpose was to assist us in becoming present.

From experience he knew that most of us would arrive with our minds filled with thoughts about our daily life. By intentionally activating our senses, we become present.

"In order to feel the tree bark," he explained, *"you must be present inside your body. To smell the fragrance of a flower, or taste the salt of the ocean, you must connect your mind and body. This tool helps to disengage you from your mental activities, and engage you in present moment awareness."*

Getting back to your senses is a powerful way to become present.

Now when I notice my mind has run ahead of itself, I intentionally activate one of my five senses. I might do something as simple as feel the ink as it flows from my pen onto a sheet of paper. Sometimes I'll pause to listen to the sound of the wind. Other times I monitor the sensation of my breathing as it moves in and out of my lungs. If I'm stuck in traffic and recognize my version of 'road rage', I place my attention in my hands and notice how the steering wheel feels. All of these activities bring me into present time and remind me to connect my mind and my body; that is, they *re-mind* me.

Simply Notice

If the experience of being present is largely unfamiliar, consider the following exercise as a way to discover the sensation of *presence*. Read through the directions first, and then see what happens when you 'simply notice'.

Place yourself in a comfortable position either standing or sitting. Close your eyes. Keeping your eyes closed, place your awareness in your right hand. Notice the subtle sensations or vibrations that exist in your right hand. It isn't necessary to do anything with these sensations other than to simply notice what they feel like.

After a few moments, shift your awareness to your left hand. Notice the subtle sensations or vibrations present in your left hand. You needn't do anything with these sensations other than notice them.

After a few moments, move your awareness to your left foot. Notice the subtle sensations or vibrations present in your left foot.

After a few moments, move your awareness to your right foot. Notice the subtle sensations or vibrations present in your right foot.

After a few moments, shift your awareness to your breathing. Notice your breath as it moves in and out of your lungs. Notice your diaphragm rising and falling. You needn't do anything other than simply notice the sensation of air moving through your body.

Take a few minutes now to complete this exercise. Notice the peace and stillness within. Notice how simple life becomes in this moment. When you feel complete with this exercise, bring your attention back to the room and continue your reading.

The sense of calm and quiet you feel might last for minutes or even hours. It's possible to access stillness and peacefulness any time you choose. Smell a flower, feel the texture of wood, listen to the sound of the birds, feel your breath, or study a beautiful object up close.

You can practice becoming present even when completing routine tasks. Feel the broom as it sweeps across the floor. Notice the slipperiness of wet soap on the dish. Feel the texture of the washcloth as you rub it across your face. The opportunities for stillness and peacefulness are all around you. It is simply a matter of becoming present.

By focusing your attention in the present, you gain the joy and peacefulness of this moment.

This is not to say that time spent remembering the past or imagining the future is not worthwhile. Quite the contrary – I described earlier how imagining the outcomes you desire assists in creating success.

The point here is to focus your attention on the past, present, and future *with conscious intention*. If you are imagining your future, then be clear on your intention in placing your awareness there. If you are immersed in a past event, recognize the purpose and consequences of living in the past.

Many people engage in a constant process of projecting their past onto the future, and as a result, miss the peace and joy of the now.

Accept that the past cannot be changed. Reliving a painful past only brings pain into your present.

Living in the Present feeds my Positive Wolf

*Evolution is a growing participation
in responsibility.*

Anonymous

Tool #4 – Choose What Does the Most Good

This next tool makes use of the power of choice. Each of us has the capacity for choice. We are able to choose not only our behaviors, but also our thoughts. I observe that most people fail to fully embrace the power of choice. They behave as though they have no choice. I described earlier how listening to our politicians, CEOs, and other leaders tell us they have no choice has convinced many of us we too have no options, and that we are consequently powerless.

Another common belief is that someone else is responsible for our life. For example, it's common for people to think others are responsible for their happiness and sadness. I often hear the expression – *"You make me happy"* and *"You make me angry."* Just as common is the question, *"How does that make you feel?"* Consistent with each of these statements is the perception of no choice.

I have come to understand that *I have the*

capacity for choice in each and every moment, and that ultimately I'm responsible for my experiences. While I cannot always control the *events* that occur in my life, I am responsible for my *response* to these events. I am responsible for the meaning I assign to the events. The word '*responsibility*' contains this message. It means having the 'ability to respond'. When I'm being responsible I am '*response-able*'. Believing I have no choice says I am not '*response-able*'.

Anger, sadness, and other forms of distress are ways of responding to events in life amongst many possibilities. If I wish more peace, happiness, and joy, it is my responsibility to choose these experiences.

Discovering Choice

An experience with my daughter taught me the power of choice. One night when Lani was fourteen years old, she ignored her normal curfew of 10 pm and instead arrived home at 4 am. In those six long hours between 10 pm and 4 am I felt many emotions coursing through my body.

Those of you with children will know exactly what they were – anger, fear, disappointment, confusion, sadness, hurt; but also love, concern, and hope. During this experience I noticed that I felt many different emotions at the same time. I now appreciate that this is the norm. In fact, people rarely experience just one emotion at a time. Rather, we feel many emotions, even some that are diametrically opposed to others. I also noticed that my emotions had different levels of intensity. Some emotions I felt quite strongly, while other emotions were less intense.

While I sat waiting for my daughter that night, I considered the many ways I might respond when she arrived home. I imagined being angry with her. I imagined expressing my surprise and disappointment. And I imagined telling her how afraid I was.

While reflecting on how I would act, it suddenly occurred to me to consider the question – *"What action of mine will do the most good?"* I have to admit that this question was new for me. I had never consciously considered whether my actions were doing the *most good*.

Instead, I realized my previous actions often depended on the intensity of my emotions at the time. If my anger was the most intense, I expressed anger. If my disappointment was the greatest, I expressed disappointment. It was as though my decision was determined by the emotion with the "highest score".

When I recognized this pattern I wondered, *"Does expressing the emotion with the highest score do the most good?"*

After some more reflecting it was clear the answer was "no". Expressing the emotion with the highest score often had negative results. With more consideration, I decided the action that would do the most good in this situation would be to express my love and gratitude that my daughter arrived home safely. Shortly after I reached this conclusion Lani arrived home. I have since laughed to myself, thinking she must have somehow sensed my thoughts, and known it was finally safe to come home. I gave her a hug and said, *"Lani, I'm glad you're home and you're safe. I love you. We'll discuss your consequence for this in the morning."*

My response surprised my daughter. Based on my previous behavior, she expected anger and judgment. This event was the beginning of a significant shift. I began to live my life differently than I had done previously. I regularly asked the question, *"What action of mine would do the most good?"*

As a result of this inquiry, my actions became more intentional and more thoughtful. I now behave in ways that are more caring, loving and positive. I experience life as my *creation*. It is now *my* life and *my* choice. I feel a sense of ownership, instead of feeling that life is being imposed on me.

To use this tool, it is necessary to consider a number of possible choices that are available and then choose the action that does the most good. I find it is best to generate at least three alternatives in any given situation. In my experience the most innovative solutions, and often the most effective, become apparent only after pushing beyond the more obvious alternatives.

Choosing the option that does the most good feeds my Positive Wolf

*The quality of your thinking
determines
the quality of your life.*

Anthony Robbins

What you resist, persists.
What you look at,
disappears.

Neale Donald Walsch

Peace Begins With Me

Tool #5 – Accept Reality

This next tool is for those times when you find yourself resisting reality. Earlier I described how resisting reality fed my negative wolf. One way to recognize if you are resisting reality is by noticing your language, specifically use of the words *should* and *shouldn't*. If you use these words frequently, it's likely you are resisting reality.

Consider the statements below:

"It shouldn't be raining now."

"It should be warmer this time of year."

"That accident should not have happened."

"My team should have won."

"I should be making more money."

"My son shouldn't have been damaged by the vaccine."

Each of these statements denies what *is*. They perpetuate a fantasy where these things either shouldn't happen or should happen. But this is not reality. Things are as they are. A "should" statement is at odds with the real world. Declaring what *should* or *shouldn't* have occurred will not change the situation. It will, however, change me into someone who is angry, frustrated, and resentful.

When something occurs that I don't like, the most positive action I can take is to *accept* it. Accept whatever it is that exists.

For years I resisted the idea of acceptance. I was uncomfortable with the notion of surrender. My resistance was based on the assumption that acceptance would cause whatever I accepted to remain unchanged. As a consequence of this belief I resisted many things.

I resisted my son's medical condition. I resisted the actions of family and friends. I resisted the decisions of colleagues and co-workers. I resisted the decisions of politicians and bureaucrats. I spent much of my life in resistance. Often my

Peace Begins With Me

resistance sounded like, *"It shouldn't be this way"*.

Slowly I became aware that my acts of resistance weren't working. They didn't take me where I wanted to go. Instead, resistance took me in the opposite direction.

I noticed that my resistance impeded change. I couldn't move forward while my attention was focused on a past event. The act of resistance is *always* about a past event because the object of my resistance already exists. Resistance is like trying to move forward while looking in a rear view mirror.

Eckhart Tolle, author of *The Power of Now* states: *"There is nothing more insane than to resist something that already exists."* Resisting reality is not creative. Instead, it frustrates, exhausts, and inhibits change. Paradoxically, the action of acceptance facilitates change. Only by fully *accepting* what is can we move on to the next step in the change process, which is to ask, *"Given this exists, what do I choose to do now?"*

Are you resisting something in your life? Are you saying, "should" or "shouldn't" to events that already exist? What do you think might happen if you simply acknowledged that these things do exist? What steps might you take then?

Byron Katie, author of the book, *Loving What Is*, presents two tools I found helpful in my quest to accept reality. Katie encourages us to do more than accept reality, she asks us to *love* reality, to love what *is*.

The first tool is a four-step process Katie calls *'The Work'*. The Work is a method of investigating reality. This is the first step in accepting reality – to know what is true. In her seminars, Katie dispenses with theory or explanations and simply invites everyone to do "the work".

She begins by handing out small index cards and invites each person to write down a complaint about someone or something. Complaints often contain statements that resist reality. Statements like: *"My husband should love me more"*,

"My boss should appreciate me more;" or *"My children should do more"*.

Then Katie asks for a volunteer. *"Who wants to do the work? Who wants to investigate reality?"*

'The Work' involves asking the following four questions:

1. *Is it true?*

2. *Are you absolutely certain it's true?*

3. *How do you react when you think this thought?*

4. *Who would you be without this thought?*

Let me provide you with an example of 'The Work'. Consider the statement: *"My wife doesn't love me."* Katie asks, *"Is this true? Is it true that your wife doesn't love you?"*

When I'm fighting with my wife, my immediate response is, *"Yes, of course it's true."* Katie then asks, *"Are you absolutely certain it's true? Can you absolutely know your wife doesn't love you?"*

When I allow myself to pause and reflect fully on Katie's question, I recognize the honest answer is, *"no"*.

"No, I can't absolutely know my wife doesn't love me." It's possible, even likely, my wife loves me as best she can at this time. It's possible my frustration has more to do with my own expectation than with her behavior. The answer to the second question is usually *"no"* – regardless of the issue a person raises.

Katie then asks her third question, *"How do you react when you think this thought? How do you feel when you think your wife doesn't love you?"* My answer is, *"I become angry, hurt, and resentful."*

Finally, Katie asks her fourth question, *"Who would you be without this thought? Who would you be without the thought – my wife doesn't love me?"*

As I reflect upon Katie's fourth question, I realize I would be more peaceful and joyful. I would be more loving and accepting.

Peace Begins With Me

As an extension of this investigation, Katie invites participants to do what she calls a *"turn-around"*. A turn-around means taking the original statement and turning it around in an attempt to identify an even deeper truth. With any given statement a number of turn-arounds are possible. In the example above, one turn-around might be: *"My wife **does** love me."* Or it could be, *"**I** don't love me"*.

Finally, Katie asks which statement among all of the statements is the most true. Often one of the turn-around statements express a deeper reality, a deeper truth.

Katie's 'Work' is a valuable tool for investigating reality. In using the tools contained in *Loving What Is,* I discovered I was often confused about what was real and what was my imagination. I came to the awareness that I frequently told myself stories that weren't true, and resisted realities that were true.

There is a second tool in Katie's book to assist in

creating more joy and happiness. Katie declares that in life there are three kinds of 'business', namely:

1. My business.

2. Your business.

3. God's business.

For those struggling with a life situation Katie asks, *"Whose business are you in?"* She believes the only business I ought to be in is *my* business. I discovered I was often involved in other people's business. When I did, the result was often a disaster. Many aspects of reality I resisted were not my business. They were someone else's business or God's business.

By asking, *"Whose business am I in?"* I stay focused on *my* business – with the result my life becomes simpler and more manageable.

Sometimes it is not clear whose business something is. In the past, many people challenged me by asking, *"If your imagination is such a power-*

ful tool, then why can't you imagine your son getting well?"

I, too, wondered about this. I now understand that my son's medical condition is not my business. It's Josh's business and God's business. My only business is how I respond to my son's medical condition.

In our society there is a tendency for people to have poor boundaries. Many people regularly confuse other people's business with their own. For example, it is common for people to believe their happiness or sadness is another's business. I often hear individuals in a relationship declare: *"You make me so happy."* While this may sound romantic, the other side of the coin is, *"You make me so unhappy."*

In my experience, neither of these statements is true. Others are *not* responsible for my emotional state. I am. When I make someone else responsible for my emotions, I eventually become angry and hurt by their failure to make me happy. And the person I have made responsible becomes frustrated and resentful.

This is because the "responsible" person has taken responsibility for something beyond their power. Just think for a moment. If we did have the power to determine another's emotional state, wouldn't we make everyone happy all of the time?

It doesn't serve either person if I take responsibility for another's business. When this happens I communicate a message that says I'm responsible for their business, with the result they stop being responsible for their business.

I believe we have an unspoken rule that says, *"There is no point in two people taking responsibility for the same thing. So, if you take responsibility, then I won't."* Life doesn't work well when people don't take responsibility for their happiness.

Are you taking responsibility for your peace, joy, and happiness? Are you attending to your business? Your happiness, peace, and joy are your responsibility. The other's happiness, peace and joy is *their* responsibility.

The first step in creating change is to accept reality. Use Byron Katie's questions as a tool to investigate reality.

Know what is true and what is the result of negative storytelling.

Stay focused on your business.

Accepting reality feeds my Positive Wolf

*As we are liberated
from our own fear
our presence automatically
liberates others.*

Nelson Mandela

Tool #6 – Trust

Another powerful tool you can use to increase your experience of peace and joy is "*trust*". I discovered that a relationship exists between fear and trust. Whenever I experience high fear, I notice that my trust is low. As I increase my trust, the fear diminishes.

This tool is about *reducing my fear by increasing my trust*.

The ability to trust enhances my capacity to experience peace and joy. It doesn't matter whom or what I trust. Simply the act of trusting reduces fear and increases peace and joy.

As part of their training, novice Buddhists are required to beg for their food. They are given an empty bowl and instructed to find their daily meal. The purpose of this ritual is to assist the young Buddhist to develop trust.

Initially the young Buddhist is filled with fear. He imagines his bowl will remain empty and he will go hungry. However, as the novice engages in this exercise, he learns to trust that his bowl will be filled. Each day, through the kindness of strangers, he is fed. Over time the young Buddhist comes to trust the universe, the abundance of life, and the compassion of others. By developing trust, he is freed to live in the present.

Now that I understand the relationship between fear and trust, I intentionally build my trust. One way I do this is by reminding myself of the things I trust each morning as I begin my day.

On the wall in my bedroom I have a list of affirmations. While dressing, I read my list and commit to trusting myself, trusting others, and trusting a higher power.

The following are examples of affirmations I regularly use:

> *I trust whatever happens to me today is*
> *for my highest good.*

> *I trust I will find a solution.*

I trust I will choose the solution that does the most good.

I trust I have enough time, energy, and money to accomplish my goals.

I am creative and adaptable.

I am succeeding.

There is value in all experiences.

The Merger

The following story illustrates the power of trust. A corporate client was involved in a merger. Management decided to hire me to prepare their employees for the emotional and psychological challenges the merger might create. Helen was encouraged to attend my seminar because she was one of the employees directly affected by the merger. At one point during the session, Helen's distress became so intense that it was difficult for her to continue.

I asked Helen if I could help her. With her consent I asked about the source of her distress. Helen angrily told me that because of the merger she was losing her job. She also declared that she would lose her home, and would be living on the streets within six months.

I asked Helen if she would share with me a few details about her life. *"How old are you?"* I asked. *"Forty-seven,"* she replied.

"How many days in forty-seven years have you lived on the street?" I inquired. *"None,"* she replied, surprised by my question.

"How many days have you gone to bed without food?" *"None,"* she replied, looking even more confused.

"Do you mean to tell me that in forty-seven years you have a 100% success rate in finding shelter and keeping yourself fed?" *"Yes, that's true,"* she replied, wondering where I was going with my questions.

Helen then demanded. *"Why are you asking me*

these silly questions?" I explained, *"It seems to me you are a pretty competent person. You have a 100% success rate in taking care of yourself for more than four decades. I'm wondering what makes you think your ability to take care of yourself will end when your job ends?"*

Helen laughed. She nodded and agreed that she was a pretty tough old gal. She proceeded to tell me stories of how she had experienced all kinds of challenges in her forty-seven years and was still here. What did I do? I simply reminded Helen that she was a competent woman and could trust herself. In my view, Helen had clearly demonstrated herself to be both resourceful and resilient. When Helen recognized this, her fear diminished.

Three Tools for Managing Fear

Thus far I have offered three tools to help manage fear. One tool is as I've just described – increase your trust. Take a few moments each day to affirm your trust. What or whom you trust is not important. It is the act of *trusting* that reduces fear.

With the understanding described earlier that telling oneself a *negative* story about a *future* event causes fear, there are two distinct tools or strategies to manage fear. One tool is to recognize that you are living in the future, and return to the present. '*Getting back to your senses*' or '*simply noticing*' are two ways of doing this. You can always manage the present.

The other tool is to change your story. If you change your negative story to a positive one, your fear will be replaced by excitement, anticipation, and enthusiasm. Become accomplished in the skill of positive story telling. Refrain from telling negative stories or allowing negative stories to be told to you. Take responsibility for your stories.

Some people comment that learning to trust is not easy. It's true that learning to trust does not occur through the occasional reading of positive statements. Learning to trust requires determination and commitment. I've come to view trust not as an 'all-or-nothing' experience, but rather as something that is grown and nurtured over time.

Learning to trust is much like strengthening a muscle. It requires regular exercise. It also requires focus. In difficult situations I've learned to ask, *"What can I trust in this moment?"* When my daughter was a teenager and prone to the antics of adolescence, I trusted that she would behave in adolescent ways. To expect otherwise was foolhardy.

Nourish your sense of trust. Avoid making general statements such as, *"I can't trust anyone"* or *"That person is not trustworthy."* Each of us has aspects of our character that are indeed worthy of trust, as well as those that are not. Focus your attention on those aspects that are worthy of trust. Build your sense of trust and your peace will increase.

Trusting feeds my Positive Wolf

If my pain could speak to me,
it would tell me . . .

Peace Begins With Me

Tool #7 – Pay Attention to Your Pain

This tool is a way of responding to pain. We all experience pain. It's a condition of being human. While the experience of pain is normal and natural, many people seemingly believe pain ought not to occur. At least, this is my interpretation based on my observation of how we typically respond to pain in our society.

The most common response we have to pain, is to medicate the pain. We medicate pain in various ways. We medicate pain with prescription medication. We also medicate with alcohol, tobacco, and marijuana. It's even possible to medicate pain through such activities as exercise, watching television, gambling, sleeping, shopping, working, and eating.

I've come to the understanding that pain has a purpose. I believe our Creator provided us with the experience of pain for a reason. Its purpose is to inform us when we are living in ways that are not healthy or life sustaining.

Unfortunately, when we medicate our pain, we diminish the opportunity to access the information communicated by the pain. Rather than inquire about the reason why the pain is there, we swallow a pill, drink the alcohol, smoke the cigarette, buy more goods, fill our stomach, or engage in numerous other ways of stopping or distracting ourselves from feeling.

When we medicate the pain, we temporarily silence the messenger and inevitably prolong the problem. This is because in silencing the messenger we fail to recognize the ways in which we are diminishing our life force.

The result is that our body is forced to resend the message, only louder. If we again medicate the pain, our body responds with an even louder message.

On and on it goes, until at some advanced stage of illness, the message is so loud we can no longer ignore it. We are forced to address the underlying cause, or die.

Peace Begins With Me

A couple of years ago I fell off a ladder while hanging Christmas decorations. I was stringing lights in a tree in front of my home when the branch my ladder was resting against suddenly gave way. The ladder lurched forward and I tumbled backward. I hit the frozen ground hard enough to fracture my spine in three places.

Fortunately the fractures did not sever my spinal cord. I was hospitalized and eventually discharged with a back brace and a prescription for pain medication.

Because of my belief in the importance of hearing the message of pain, I chose not to fill the prescription. Instead, I allowed myself to feel pain. I healed quickly and completely, and the doctor remarked at the speed of my recovery. I attribute my rapid healing to my willingness to listen to the message contained in pain.

After lying on my back for a while I'd feel well enough to stand and walk around. Initially I could walk only a few steps before the pain sent me back to my bed. A few hours later I'd again feel well enough to stand and walk around. This time I was able to be on my feet a longer period before the pain presented itself. Again, I honored its message and returned to my bed.

Over the following days and weeks I repeated this cycle of lying in bed, feeling well enough to get up, walking for a period of time, experiencing pain, and returning to bed.

At the beginning my recovery seemed slow based on the brief amount of time I could stand. In a few weeks, however, I was upright and walking without pain most of the time.

By listening to the message my body sent, I avoided pushing my body beyond the limits of the healing.

Had I taken the medication as prescribed, I would have been able to be on my feet for longer periods of time – but in all likelihood would have caused further injury to my back and thus prolonged my condition.

If My Pain Could Speak to Me

When I work with clients in my counselling practice I regularly invite them to *pay attention to their pain*. One way I do this is by asking them to write the following statement at the top of a blank sheet of paper: *"If my pain could speak to me, it would tell me . . ."* I ask them to complete the statement as a homework assignment.

Invariably clients return with valuable information. Many have recorded statements as: *"My pain tells me to slow down, to let go, or to find another way."* This valuable information is available if we take the time to listen.

This same principle holds true for emotional pain. In my experience emotional pain is the result of holding onto beliefs, expectations, or ideas that aren't true. During the first few years of my son's life I experienced incredible emotional pain.

Eventually I discovered that I was holding onto many ideas and beliefs that weren't true.

When I released these untrue beliefs, my emotional pain dissipated.

One of the false beliefs I held was I couldn't be happy until my son stopped seizing. After nearly two decades of uncontrolled seizing, I finally acknowledged that it was foolish for me to continue connecting my happiness to my son's medical condition. I realized these two events – my happiness and my son's medical condition – were not connected except in my own mind. By letting go of this untrue belief, my emotional pain went away.

Notice the role of pain in your life. See if you can discover the message embedded in the pain. Consider whether you are holding onto beliefs, stories, or ideas that are not true. Explore what happens when you let go of these false beliefs.

When I pay attention to my Pain, I feed my Positive Wolf

*What are the ways
you medicate
your pain?*

Worry is interest paid
on trouble
before it becomes due.

Dean Inge

Tool #8 – Schedule Worry Time

Of all the tools in my toolbox, scheduling worry time is the simplest and yet most powerful.

All of us worry. Most people worry far too often. While we have all been advised not to worry, most are unable to follow this simple advice. I discovered that scheduling worry time is advice I can follow. While this idea might sound strange, let me remind you that the right answer is the one that works. If you wish to reduce the amount of time you spend worrying, consider using this tool.

The intention of this tool is to reduce the amount of time you spend worrying and to increase the efficiency of your worry. Research indicates most worry involves the same thoughts over and over.

The first step is to decide how long you wish to worry each day. Don't say you don't wish to worry because, at least at the present time, you seem to have a need to worry. Ten to fifteen minutes daily is usually plenty of time. Next, decide when and where you will worry. It's important you select a specific time and place to do your worrying.

The way you implement this strategy is the following:

At the start of your day remind yourself of your worry time and place. I remind myself: *"Today I will worry between 7:00 and 7:15 pm, sitting in the red chair in the living room."* Then, as you go about your day, notice if you are worrying outside of your scheduled worry time.

Whenever this happens, gently remind yourself of your worry time and place. Your mind will release the worry thought and become quiet again. Later, if you notice yourself worrying once again, remind yourself of your scheduled worry time. Finally, at the appointed time, sit in your worry place and begin worrying for the period you have agreed.

During the first few days of implementing

this strategy, it's likely you will catch yourself worrying dozens of times outside of your worry time. For those of you who are good worriers, you might even catch yourself hundreds of times. Be assured that as the days progress, the amount of worrying outside of your scheduled time will diminish. After using this tool for just one week, your mind will respond to the imposed structure and become quieter.

This strategy works because your mind is receptive to direction. The truth is most people don't give their mind the kind of direction it can follow. Telling oneself *"Don't worry"* does not work. Saying *"I'll worry later"* is not precise enough for your mind. When you give your mind specific instructions and honor these instructions by being true to your word (sitting down in your worry chair at the appointed time), your mind will respond beautifully.

Scheduling worry time feeds my Positive Wolf

In the end it is the ability to change,
to look at things in a new way,
which distinguishes
those who are happy,
from those who are not.

Anonymous

Tool #9 – Be Happy Now

Many people are under the illusion happiness is dependent upon *external* events, events such as what others think, do, or say, and what happens or doesn't happen in the physical world.

For many years I believed this too. For many years I was happy when my son was free of seizures, and unhappy when he'd begin seizing again. I lived as though I had no control over my happiness. Today I recognize the fallacy of this way of thinking. I now understand that happiness is an *inside* job rather than an *outside* job.

Happiness is a decision. Happiness is a choice. I choose to be happy or not, in each and every moment. Abraham Lincoln is accredited with saying, *"Most people are about as happy as they make up their minds to be."* He didn't say people are as happy as their partners, children, neighbors, or employers make them. He said happiness is the result of something that occurs in one's mind. I create my happiness or unhappiness by my thoughts, specifically by the meaning I assign to the events in my life. The label I assign to life's events determines my experience. By taking responsibility for the meaning I assign, I experience more happiness.

I also described earlier how I fed my negative wolf by delaying my happiness, by placing my happiness in the future rather than the present. The shortest path to happiness is to be happy *now*. Not after the mortgage is paid off. Not after the children leave home. Not when the weekend comes, or the holidays, or after winning a lottery. Living with the belief: *"I'll be happy when . . ."* places obstacles between happiness and the present. I now appreciate I can remove these obstacles anytime I choose, and thus experience happiness *now*.

Once I fully accept the notion that happiness is my responsibility and is dependent upon my thoughts, there is no sane reason why I would continue to deprive myself of happiness. Now, whenever I feel anger or sadness, I pause and ask, *"Do I want to experience this emotion, or would I rather do something about this?"* I can choose to continue with my experience of anger or sadness, or I can change my thoughts, and experience happiness again. The choice is mine. My friend Peter states: *"If happiness is your goal then you need to be as committed to happiness as with any other goal."*

I'm reminded of the story of a young Buddhist devotee seated at the feet of his Master. The student inquires of his Master, *"Master, how will I know when I have arrived?"* The wise Master replies, *"You will have arrived when you shift from seeking happiness to creating happiness."*

Heroic figures such as Nelson Mandela have demonstrated the power of the mind to create happiness even while imprisoned in a jail cell. Learn to embrace your power. Create your happiness in each and every moment. Happiness is within your power.

Choosing to be happy Now feeds my Positive Wolf

The way you breathe
is the way
you live your life.

Dr. John Travis, M.D.

Tool #10 – Breathe from Your Diaphragm

One final tool for your consideration is the reminder to breathe using your diaphragm. Those involved in martial arts, yoga, singing, weightlifting, Pilates, and other similar practices will already know the significance of breathing from your diaphragm. If you are not familiar with these disciplines you might wonder, *"Why is it important to breathe from your diaphragm?"*

Breathing is the most important activity we do. When we stop breathing, we die. Breathing fills us with the energy of life. Proper breathing inspires us both physically and metaphorically.

Let me share with you the story of when I first discovered the importance of diaphragmatic breathing. A number of years ago I attended a workshop on breathing. The facilitator asked us to sit on the floor, cross our legs, and close our eyes. He then asked us to worry about something. As we sat worrying the facilitator walked around the room and pushed each of us over.

Now that he had our full attention, he began his lecture. *"Most of you do not live in your body. You spend most of your life in your mind and drag your physical body around as though it has no value. Today, I'm going to teach you to live in your body again. By the end of the day, you will breathe the way you were meant to breathe."*

Our instructor then described the body's physical design. He explained how our breathing apparatus is similar to an old fashioned bellows that is used to fan a fire. By separating the handles of the bellows a vacuum is created. This causes air to be drawn in. Squeezing the handles together pushes the air out.

"Your diaphragm and lungs work in exactly the same way. When you open your diaphragm a vacuum is created in your lungs, causing oxygen to be drawn in. Closing the diaphragm pushes the carbon dioxide out."

He then asked us to recall how a newborn baby breathes. We all acknowledged that when a baby breathes its belly rises and falls. A baby instinctively uses its diaphragm to breathe. If we are breathing properly our belly ought to rise and fall also. When most adults breathe, however, their belly remains flat. All movement occurs in their chest rather than their diaphragm. The result is an inadequate supply of oxygen.

Once the instructor explained the mechanics of proper breathing, and checked to ensure we were doing so, he invited us to again sit on the floor with crossed legs and closed eyes. This time, when he attempted to push us over, he was unable to do so.

By changing our breathing we were re-connected with our body. We became more stable and grounded. By grounded I mean centered, solid, resilient, and not easily knocked over. This is true for our emotional and psychological bodies as well.

I explain to my clients that changing the way they breathe changes them from a *'sponge'* to a '*duck*.' I notice that when a person breathes using their lungs only, their life resembles that of a sponge. They absorb the struggles and challenges of life. Over time they become saturated and heavy and have difficulty moving forward. I believe many people who experience depression do so in part because of improper breathing.

When a person breathes using their diaphragm, the struggles and challenges of life roll off his or her back. As a result, they stay light and buoyant, and float through life like a duck. When I feel heavy with life I remind myself to breathe from my diaphragm and to become like a duck.

An easy way to notice if you are breathing using your diaphragm is to lie on your back, loosen your clothing, and place your hands on your lower belly. When breathing properly your hands will rise and fall with each breath. If your hands stay in one position, then you're breathing with your lungs only.

Many people are curious as to the reason why we stop using our diaphragm to breathe. One explanation is that our society finds a flat stomach more attractive than a round stomach. Children are encouraged to pull in their stomach. Fashion designers design clothing to fit snugly at the waist. From my perspective, however, the reason has more to do with the prevalence of negative stories in our society. As discussed earlier, telling negative stories creates the experience of fear. When in a state of fear, our body instinctively shifts into survival mode. This means we prepare for fight or flight. Both actions require the tensing of our muscles.

Living with chronic fear means that we keep our muscles tight. As a consequence, breathing from our diaphragm becomes compromised.

Eyes Wide Shut

During the breathing seminar I discovered something else about the power of diaphragmatic breathing. The instructor invited us to stand, close our eyes and breathe using our diaphragm. He then asked us to run around the room as fast as we could in any direction, all the while keeping our eyes closed.

What do you imagine happened when a dozen people began running around a room with their eyes closed? You might have guessed that we quickly collided with one another creating a giant pile of bodies on the floor.

In fact, the opposite occurred. Not one person got knocked over. Amazingly, there weren't any collisions at all! Each of us successfully navigated our way around the room with our eyes closed. This result greatly surprised every participant, including me. What had just occurred didn't seem possible. Yet, we had just done it.

Before explaining, the instructor invited us to repeat the exercise, this time with our eyes open. To my further astonishment, I discovered I could not move more than a few steps without colliding with another person, even though my eyes were open. As I stepped away from this person, I invariably collided with another.

Sensing our confusion, the instructor laughed. *"The problem,"* he stated, *"is you think that your intellect is so smart. Yet, by closing your eyes so that you cannot use your intellect, you are able to do something that cannot be done with your eyes open."*

"You are able to successfully navigate the room with your eyes closed because there is wisdom in your body far superior to your intellect. You access this wisdom when you close your eyes and breathe from your diaphragm."

Not long after this surprising experience I read the biography of Albert Einstein. I learned Einstein's ideas didn't come to him while at his desk in his office. Instead, the new and innovative ideas Einstein is famous for came to him as he walked in the woods each day. I suspect Einstein knew how to access the wisdom within.

Notice your breathing as you go about your

day. Notice whether you are breathing from the top of your lungs or using your diaphragm. Allow your belly to rise and fall. Notice the difference this makes in your life.

See if you change from being a sponge to being a duck. See if you access an inner wisdom.

Breathing from my Diaphragm feeds my Positive Wolf

*Unless you change
your direction,
you will end up
where you are headed.*

Chinese Proverb

Peace Begins With Me

Chapter Five

Personal Action Plan

When I began this book I shared with you these principles of success:

> **Progress** – *requires doing something different from what you are currently doing.*

> **Insanity** – *is doing the same and expecting a different outcome.*

In order to progress you must do something different from what you are currently doing. In the space below I invite you to list three new strategies, tools, or activities you commit to doing in the coming week.

This is an opportunity to take a step forward, a step toward a life of increased peace and joy. This is an opportunity to feed the positive wolf.

Three things I will do differently this week are:

1. _____

_____

2. _____

_____

3. _____

_____

Rate of Retention

As I mentioned earlier I was an Instructor at a local community college. One of my discoveries from this experience was just how little information students actually retain. My own experience as a teacher confirmed what scientific research has shown – the rate of retention of new information depends upon the method of instruction.

When information is given:	*We retain:*
Verbally	10%
In writing	15%
Verbally and written	20%

Given that the information contained in this book is presented in written form, most readers will retain approximately 15% of the information. More importantly it means 85% will be forgotten within two months. The fact is that simply reading this book will yield limited results.

There is another method of instruction that yields significantly higher rates of retention. This method is *sharing*. Research confirms that if a student undertakes to share new information with at least one other individual, the rate of retention increases substantially. Sharing causes the rate of retention to rise to approximately 90%.

If you are an average reader, you have invested approximately three to four hours reading this book. If you want your time to be well spent, if you want to retain 90% of the information, and if you are serious about becoming more peaceful and joyful, I encourage you to share your newly acquired knowledge with another. In the space below, identify one person with whom you will share this information in the next week.

I will share the information contained in this

book with _____

by this date _____.

How Change Happens

As you travel on this journey of change it's important to have an appreciation for how change happens. My concern is that if you have an unrealistic expectation, then the pace of change might discourage you and cause you to abandon your quest. The following is a unique way of describing change. I have found it a helpful metaphor to understand the pace of change.

Change occurs in the following way:

You walk down a street. At the end of the street is a manhole to access the underground services in the neighborhood. The cover has been removed from the manhole. You are too distracted to notice the cover is missing and you fall into the hole.

After your initial shock, you climb out of the hole and continue on your way.

The next day you walk down the same street. Again, the cover has been removed from the manhole. Again, you fail to notice the cover is missing. You fall into the hole. You climb out of the hole and continue on your way.

On the third day you walk down the same street. Again, the cover has been removed from the manhole. This time you notice the cover is missing, yet still manage to fall into the hole. You climb out of the hole and continue on your way.

On the fourth day you walk down the same street. Once again the cover is missing from the manhole. This time you notice and successfully step around the hole. You continue on your way.

On the fifth day you walk down a different street.

My experience of change is like this. I often fall into holes and don't see how I got there. Eventually I climb out of the hole and continue on my way. Gradually I begin to see the holes in my life, yet still manage to fall into them.

Over time I recognize some of the holes with enough foresight to step away from them.

Eventually I choose to walk a different path. A path that is more peaceful and joyful.

I share this metaphor with you to support you in your efforts to change your life. Change doesn't happen all at once. It happens gradually, step by step.

The tools described in this book will assist you to walk a different path, one that is more peaceful and joyful. Happy traveling.

You're the one
you've been waiting for.

Byron Katie

Peace Begins With Me

Chapter Six

Peace Begins With Me

My deepest intention in writing this book is to increase the experience of peace on this planet. It is my hope and desire that *all* people come to a better understanding of how to live in peace, and in doing so, experience peace.

When I observe the world today it seems the ability to live peacefully with one another is the aspect of humanity most in need of improvement. I believe all of us desire peace. All of us deserve peace. Yet, for most, peace is elusive. This is because we lack the knowledge of how to live peacefully.

When I practice the tools and strategies contained in this book, strategies as: taking responsibility for the meaning I assign to events, using my imagination creatively, living in the present, choosing what does the most good, paying attention to my pain, managing my worry time, trusting, accepting reality, being happy now, and breathing from my diaphragm, I experience greater peace. I enjoy this experience of peace.

I believe that if we are to experience peace on this planet, it must begin within.

Peace begins with me. Once I have mastered peace within, only then will I experience peace in my family, my community, my country, and finally, the world.

There is another reason I invited you to share the ideas contained in this book. My hope is that by sharing this information with others, your efforts and this knowledge will contribute toward greater peace on this planet. There is an urgent need for peace at this time.

I believe teaching the skills of peacemaking is *the* most important work we can do right now. I invite you to be an agent of peace.

As you work, as you play, as you think, and as you love, do so with peace in your heart.

If I am at war with myself,
I can bring little peace
to my fellow man.

Anonymous

Peace Begins With Me

10 Ways
To Create Peace & Joy

1. Take responsibility for assigning meaning.

2. Use your imagination creatively.

3. Live in the present.

4. Choose what does the most good.

5. Pay attention to your pain.

6. Schedule worry time.

7. Trust.

8. Accept reality.

9. Be happy now.

10. Breathe from your diaphragm.

The battle of my heart
will be won by the wolf
that wins the battle
of every man's heart.
It is the wolf I feed.

Native Story

Bibliography

The following people and their writings contributed to the ideas contained in *Peace Begins With Me*:

Al Etmanski
A Good Life, 2004

Byron Katie,
Loving What Is, 2002

Deepak Chopra
The Seven Spiritual Laws of Success, 1994.

Don Miguel Ruiz
The Four Agreements, 1997

Eckhart Tolle
Practicing the Power of Now, 2002.
Stillness Speaks, 2003.

Lee Johnson
How to Escape Your Comfort Zones.
Penguin Books, 1995.

Neale Donald Walsch
Conversations With God, 1994.

Ray Woollam
Have a Plain Day, 1989.
On Choosing With a Quiet Mind, 1985.

Ross Buchanan
Life Without Limits, 2000.

Peace Begins With Me:
The Workshop

by Ross Buchanan, CEO
Strategic Results International

Over the years I have had the opportunity to watch Ted deliver his workshop version of this book to hundreds of clients.

I call it an "opportunity" because in the 20 years I have been involved in Professional Development, seldom have I seen people "get it" the way they do in Ted's seminar.

And what do they get?

Peace.

Beautiful, simple, serene peace.

Exactly what many people consumed by the chaos of the today's business world are searching for – to find peace and to keep it.

As I read *Peace Begins With Me* it felt just like being present at one of Ted's workshops. Without a doubt much of the magic of the workshop is found in this book.

If you would like Ted to present
Peace Begins With Me - The Workshop
to your company or organization, you can contact him at tjkuntz@axion.net or visit his website at www.peacebeginswithme.ca

About the Author

Ted Kuntz is a psychotherapist in private practice in Vancouver Canada. Yet the wisdom he shares in this book didn't come from his formal training. It came from his personal journey as the father of a disabled child. This deeply personal story is an inspiration to all of us who want to move past pain and return to peace and joy.

Ted is actively involved in his community creating new stories about people with a disability and other marginalized people and thus changing the way we see one other. His passion is to help create a more peaceful world where we all belong.

Ted is highly pursued to share his stories and present his wisdom to a wide variety of audiences from social services to the corporate world.

To Order Additional Copies of Peace Begins With Me

Order via email:

Contact Ted Kuntz at *tjkuntz@axion.net*

Order by mail:

Send a cheque for $30.70 CAN ($24.95 plus shipping and GST) to:

Ted Kuntz
201–3041 Anson Avenue
Coquitlam, B.C. V3B 2H6
Discounts for orders of 6 copies and more

To identify a bookstore in your community that carries *Peace Begins With Me*, view Ted's website at *www.peacebeginswithme.ca*

If you are a not-for-profit organization and would like to use *Peace Begins With Me* as an opportunity to raise funds for your organization, please contact Ted at *tjkuntz@axion.net*

Resources for Families who have a Relative with a Disability

When you have a child with a disability, your life changes. As a parent, sibling, or grandparent, it takes courage and vision to author a new story.

It takes assistance to 'feed the positive wolf'.

Planned Lifetime Advocacy Network Society (PLAN) is a family led organization that has been instrumental in assisting me to create new dreams and hopes for Joshua's future.

PLAN is internationally recognized for its innovation in creating 'a good life' for people with a disability, for facilitating 'networks of support', and for ensuring a safe and secure future for our loved ones.

PLAN has produced a number of valuable resources for families. They include:

–   *A Good Life by Al Etmanski*

–   *Peace of Mind - interactive DVD*

–   *Safe and Secure - Al Etmanski, Vickie Cammack, & Jack Collins*

–   *In the Company of Others - a photo documentary of networks of support*

To learn more about PLAN, and to subscribe to Planfacts, their quarterly newsletter, visit PLAN's website at:

www.plan.ca <http://www.plan.ca>

or call 604-439-9566.